The Handbook of the

Michael G. Kort

Twenty-First Century Books
Brookfield, Connecticut

Photographs courtesy of © K. R. Downey Photography: p. 16; © Liaison Agency: pp. 19 (Marek Skorupski/Gamma Pologne), 28 (Patrick Piel), 140 (Francis Li), 190 (Hulton Getty); Sovfoto/Eastfoto: p. 37; © Impact Visuals: pp. 47 (1990 Larry Boyd), 52 (Sean Sprague), 189 (Larry Boyd); © Woodfin Camp & Associates: p. 58 (Adam Woolfitt); HIAS: p 67; © Trip: pp. 79 (B. Gibbs), 230 (G. Spenceley), 231 (I. Wellbelove), 240 (M. Barlow); © Corbis: p. 86 (Peter Turnley); The Image Finders: p. 91; © Corbis/Sygma: pp. 93 (J. Groch), 218 (Ewa Grochowiak), 219 (Patrick Durand); AP/Wide World Photos: pp. 108, 183, 198, 202 (top), 203, 209, 210, 216, 217, 220, 221 (top), 227, 228, 229, 232, 235; Reuters/Bettmann: p. 123; Library of Congress: p. 126; Reuters/Archive Photos: pp. 161 (Yannis Behrakis), 191 (Pawel Kopczynski), 197 (Mike Blake), 202 (bottom, Francois Walschaets), 204 (Stevo Vasiljevic), 213 (Petar Kujundzic), 214 (Sean Gallup), 221 (bottom, Petar Kujundzic), 223 (Larry Downing), 233 (Arben Celi), 236 (Hrvoje Polan), 241 (Sean Gallup); NGS Image Collection: pp. 186 (Raymond K. Gehman), 194 (James Stanfield); Popperfoto/Archive Photos: p. 206; © Tony Stone Images/Anthony Cassidy: pp. 226, 239

Maps by Joe LeMonnier

Flags courtesy of The Flag Research Center, Winchester, MA.

Library of Congress Cataloging-in-Publication Data
Kort, Michael, 1944–
The handbook of the new Eastern Europe/Michael G. Kort.
p. cm.
Includes bibliographical references and index.
ISBN 0–7613–1362–1 (lib. bdg.)
1. Europe, Eastern. 2. Europe, Central. I. Title
DJK9.K67 2001
943—dc21 00-57708

Published by Twenty-First Century Books
A Division of The Millbrook Press
2 Old New Milford Road
Brookfield, CT 06804
www.millbrookpress.com

Text copyright © 2001 by Michael G. Kort

For Bonnie

**dear friend to Carol and me
and godmother
to Eleza and Tamara**

Contents

The Handbook of the

New

Eastern

Europe

Chapter One

What Is Eastern Europe?

On March 5, 1946, less than a year after the Allied victory over Nazi Germany and the end of World War II, former British Prime Minister Winston Churchill traveled to Fulton, Missouri, to speak about the situation in Europe. He came as the guest of President Harry S. Truman. Churchill's message for his American audience was grim:

> From Stettin in the Baltic to Trieste in the Adriatic, an iron curtain has descended across the continent. Behind that line lie all the capitals of the ancient states of central and eastern Europe. Warsaw, Berlin, Prague, Vienna, Budapest, Belgrade, Bucharest, and Sofia, all these famous cities and the population around them lie in the Soviet sphere and all are subject, in one form or another, not only to Soviet influence but to a very high and increasing measure of control from Moscow.[1]

Aside from warning the American people about the dangerous developments in Europe, Churchill in effect gave them what may have been the first definition of the region that soon would be called "Eastern Europe." Ultimately, post–World War II Eastern Europe took shape a bit differently than Churchill described in his famous "Iron Curtain" speech. Vienna, capital of the "ancient state" of Austria, did not end up as part of Eastern Europe. At the same time, political developments placed Tirana, the capital of Albania and a city not mentioned by Churchill, behind the Iron Curtain.

As Churchill's Iron Curtain speech indicates, the term Eastern Europe, at least as it has been used since 1946, is defined more by politics than by geography. It refers to the part of Europe immediately to the west of the former Soviet Union that was under Communist control from the end of World War II until 1989. This region includes a large chunk of what before 1945 generally was called "Central Europe." It also includes most of the area called "Southeastern Europe," or the Balkan Peninsula. Making matters more complicated, "Eastern Europe" in a strict geographical sense is not the eastern part of the European continent. It actually lies near the center of Europe, sandwiched between Western Europe, which extends westward to the Atlantic Ocean, and the vast plain once controlled by the former Soviet Union, which stretches eastward toward the Ural Mountains where Europe and Asia meet.

Eastern Europe is also partially defined by the complicated relationships among the peoples who live there. Over the centuries shifts in power have redrawn national borders, fractured and reassembled countries, and separated and then driven various groups of people together. These upheavals have left the region with a tangled and twisted ethnic makeup, with multiple ethnic groups squeezed uncomfortably into a single national unit and other ethnic groups split apart by several international borders. On a personal level, this has blurred and confused identities and created mixed and sometimes conflicting loyalties. Odon von Horvath, a well-known author between World Wars I and II, used his personal background to illustrate Eastern Europe's complex and intricate ethnic web:

If you ask me what is my native country, I answer: I was born in Fiume, I grew up in Belgrade, Budapest, Pressburg, Vienna, and Munich, and I have a Hungarian passport; but I have no fatherland. I am very much a mix of old Austria-Hungary: at once Magyar, Croatian, German, and Czech; my country is Hungary, my mother tongue is German.[2]

Outsiders often have had only a vague knowledge of Eastern Europe. When American students study Eastern Europe, frequently it is only to learn about its troubled history and not to understand what the people of the region have achieved. This certainly was true during the twentieth century, when the sparks that ignited two world wars were first struck in Eastern Europe. In June 1914 the assassination of Austria's Archduke Ferdinand in the city of Sarajevo began the crisis that led to the outbreak of World War I a month later. On September 1, 1939, Nazi Germany's invasion of Poland began World War II. Finally, as the guns of that dreadful war were just falling silent, the Cold War that divided the world for more than four decades began as the Soviet Union imposed its control over Eastern Europe.

It was, in fact, the Cold War between the United States and the Soviet Union, which dominated international affairs from about 1945 to 1990, that fused parts of "Central" and "Southeastern" Europe into a single region called "Eastern Europe." During the Cold War era, Eastern Europe was composed of eight countries: East Germany, Poland, Czechoslovakia, Hungary, Romania, Bulgaria, Yugoslavia, and Albania. Today three of those countries—East Germany, Yugoslavia, and Czechoslovakia—no longer exist. They disappeared from the map shortly after Communist control of Eastern Europe collapsed in 1989. In 1990, East Germany, an artificial Soviet creation to begin with, was absorbed by West Germany to form a reunited Germany. The multicultural country of Yugoslavia disintegrated in 1991, a victim of ethnic tensions and rivalries.

Its death in turn gave birth, at times violently, to five new countries: Croatia, Slovenia, Macedonia, Bosnia-Herzegovena, and a new Yugoslavia consisting of Serbia and Montenegro. Ethnic conflict immediately tore apart Bosnia-Herzegovena and plunged it into civil war; it exists officially on the map only because of the presence of United Nations peacekeeping forces. Czechoslovakia, another multicultural country, in 1993 divided peacefully into two new nations, the Czech Republic and the Slovak Republic.

These changes left twelve countries in Eastern Europe: Poland, Hungary, the Czech Republic, the Slovak Republic, Romania, Bulgaria, Albania, Slovenia, Croatia, Macedonia, the Federal Republic of Yugoslavia (Serbia and Montenegro), and Bosnia-Herzegovena. They share a common recent past of more than four decades of Communist rule. They also face a common challenge of building democratic free-market societies in the face of serious social, economic, and environmental problems. At the same time, these countries are the heirs to a variety of cultural, political, and historical traditions that have left some of them far better equipped than others to cope with their problems. At one end of the spectrum are Poland, Hungary, and the Czech Republic, all of which have made substantial progress in rebuilding their societies since 1989. At the other end are most of the countries of the former Yugoslavia, where warfare, ethnic turmoil, and other disturbances have blocked progress or often made conditions worse. Overall, while Eastern Europe now has emerged from the shadow of its Communist past, many difficulties, both old and new, continue to cloud the region's future.

The Geographic Setting

Eastern Europe is an area of about 450,000 square miles (1.2 million square kilometers), about three-quarters the size of the state of Alaska. It stretches approximately 1,000 miles (1,600 kilometers) north to south from the Baltic Sea to the borders of

Greece and Turkey. From west to east it is between 250 and 500 miles (between 400 and 800 kilometers) across.

Eastern Europe has natural boundaries only where it touches the Baltic, Black, or Adriatic seas. It is largely an inland region. All of Eastern Europe has only 1,500 miles (2,400 kilometers) of coastline along the Baltic, Black, and Adriatic seas. This short coastline, less than the ocean shoreline of France, has few natural harbors. As a result, the countries of Eastern Europe have had to rely on seaports controlled by outside powers to carry much of their trade. At the same time, Eastern Europe's lack of natural boundaries to the east or west has left it exposed to invaders. That geographic disadvantage helps explain the turbulence that for many centuries has marked the region's history.

Eastern Europe is divided into three primary geographic areas. Its northern section is part of the enormous North European Plain that runs from the Atlantic Ocean, where Europe begins, to the Ural Mountains, where Europe ends. The same lowland extends more than 1,000 miles farther east into the heart of Asia. The North European Plain, which varies from about 250 to about 350 miles in width, rarely rises more than 300 feet (91 meters) above sea level. Two major rivers, the Vistula and the Oder, cross through the region as they flow northward to the Baltic Sea. The southern boundary of the North European Plain in Eastern Europe is formed by, from west to east, the Sudeten and Carpathian mountain ranges.

The second major geographic region of Eastern Europe is the drainage area of the Danube River, or the Danube Basin. The core of this region is the Plain of Hungary. Highlands form the northwestern boundary of the Danube Basin. Elsewhere the basin is ringed by mountain ranges: the Dinaric Alps in the southwest, the Carpathian Mountains in the north and east, and the Balkan Mountains and Transylvanian Alps respectively in the south and north after the Danube cuts through the Carpathians and flows into the Balkan Peninsula and through a second broad plain en route to the Black Sea.

A view of the Balkan Mountains in Bulgaria

Eastern Europe's third major geographic area is the Balkan Peninsula. "Balkan" is the Turkish word for mountains, and it aptly describes the 200,000-square-mile (518,000-square-kilometer) region. With the exception of the broad plain in Romania that is part of the Danube Basin, most of the Balkan Peninsula is mountainous.

Despite its rugged terrain, the Balkan Peninsula for thousands of years has been a magnet for invaders. It borders on five seas and is cut by natural highways formed by river valleys. Wedged between the Middle East and the heart of Europe, the Balkan Peninsula has long been a battleground for powerful states from Asia, Europe, and the Middle East. Waves of invasions over many centuries have left the peninsula with a complicated and often explosive mixture of peoples. The inability of those groups to get along has played an important part in the region's troubled history.

Most of Eastern Europe has what is called a "continental" climate of cold, snowy winters and warm, rainy summers. It is a climate similar to that of the midwestern United States. During the cold winters rivers freeze and snowfall is heavy. The plain regions are whipped by bone-chilling winds. The main exception to this rule is in the south along the coasts of the Adriatic and Black seas, where a "Mediterranean" climate of mild winters and warm, dry summers prevails.

The Peoples of Eastern Europe

About 140 million people live in Eastern Europe. Most of them belong to about a dozen major national and ethnic groups. The great majority of Eastern Europe's population are Slavs, which means they speak one of the Slavic family of languages. The Slavs, whose original homeland probably was along the Vistula River in Poland, began migrating to other parts of Eastern Europe in the sixth century. The Slavs of Eastern Europe eventually divided into two main groups: Western and Southern. The Poles, Czechs, and Slovaks are Western Slavs. The Serbs, Croats, Slovenes, Bulgarians, Montenegrins, and Macedonians are Southern Slavs. The largest group of Slavs, the Eastern Slavs, do not live in Eastern Europe. The Eastern Slavs, made up of Russians, Ukrainians, and Belarusians, live farther east in countries that once were part of the former Soviet Union.

There are also significant non-Slavic groups in Eastern Europe. The Romanians, Hungarians (or Magyars), and Albanians are the non-Slavic peoples that have their own nations. The Romanians are descendants of the Vlach people, a group of tribes whose origins are uncertain, but who probably lived in the western part of the Balkan Peninsula in ancient times. They speak a Latin-based language similar to French or Italian, although over the centuries Romanian has picked up many Slavic words. The Hungarians were the last of the major peoples of Eastern Europe to arrive in the region. They were skilled horsemen who burst into Eastern Europe from Asia late in the ninth century. Eventually they settled on the plain that today bears their name. The Albanians are descendants of the Illyrians, who in ancient times lived along the coast of the Adriatic Sea.

There are two groups that played major roles in Eastern European life for about a thousand years but today are present in the region only in small numbers: the Germans and the Jews. The Jews came to the region as settlers, while the Germans arrived both as settlers and conquerors. Both groups established communities throughout the region. The Jewish presence in Eastern Europe was almost eliminated as a result of the Holocaust, Nazi Germany's campaign to exterminate the Jews of Europe during World War II. The majority of the Jews who survived the Holocaust eventually emigrated, mainly to Israel, leaving only remnants of a community that once was an important part of almost every Eastern European country.

Millions of Germans lived in Eastern Europe prior to World War II. Most lived in territory that at the time was part of Germany, although large communities existed in several other countries. After World War II, as the world reacted in horror to the crimes of Nazi Germany and as international borders were redrawn, about ten million Germans were forced to move. The largest number were driven from territory detached from Germany and turned over to Poland. The Soviet Union annexed a small section of eastern Germany and expelled its population. Other Germans had to leave a mountainous section of Czechoslovakia along the border with Germany called the Sudetenland, as well as parts of Hungary, Romania, and Yugoslavia. These displaced Germans settled inside the new and smaller borders of either West or East Germany.

A gypsy tent, photographed in Romania in 1992

A third group, the Gypsies, has also lived in Eastern Europe for centuries. The Gypsies are a nomadic people who originally came from India. While Gypsies are present in every Eastern European country, their largest communities are in Hungary and Romania.

Three Historical Benchmarks

Several major historical developments have had an enormous impact on the history of Eastern Europe. One involves religious divisions. In the eleventh century, a split between the Catholic Church based in Rome and the Eastern Orthodox Church based in Constantinople divided the Christian world. Most of Eastern Europe fell on the Roman Catholic side of that line. However, in the Balkan Peninsula that line shifts to the west, dividing the lands of the former Yugoslavia in half. Over the centuries the Catholic/Orthodox border has been the scene of many conflicts; the latest tragic example can be seen today in Bosnia. A second religious frontier runs through the Balkans, this one separating the Christian and Islamic worlds. That line, which continues eastward into Asia, also has been the source of frequent strife.

Another distinctive feature of Eastern Europe is that for several hundred years most of the region was ruled by foreign empires: the Hapsburg Empire (controlled by ethnic Germans and called the Austrian Empire after 1806), the Russian Empire, and the Ottoman (or Turkish) Empire. This retarded the development of local traditions of self-government. There were other negative legacies as well. These empires forced people with different languages, cultures, and traditions to live within the same political borders, while doing nothing to promote intergroup tolerance and understanding. Furthermore, five centuries of Ottoman rule over the Balkan Peninsula increased the differences between the Balkans and the parts of Eastern Europe associated with Western European culture.

A third development that has deeply affected the status of Eastern Europe is the pattern of economic change in Europe as a whole. At the close of the Middle Ages, the societies of Western Europe began a rapid process of economic, political, and social modernization. That progress did not extend into Eastern Europe. Ever since, Eastern Europe has had to struggle to overcome its condition of "backwardness," both in terms of economic prosperity and lack of political democracy.

The Major Periods of Eastern European History

The history of Eastern Europe before 1989 can loosely be divided into six major periods. The first period dates roughly from the second to the ninth centuries. Mass migrations changed the population of the many parts of the region. The migrations began in the third century, when nomadic Germanic tribes moved into territory south of the Danube controlled by the Roman Empire. These tribes continued their migrations until they finally settled in Western Europe. After later invasions by Turkic tribes from Asia, beginning with the fierce Huns who burst into Europe late in the fourth century, Slavs began the migrations in which they spread over much of Eastern Europe. Their occupation of new lands was part of a larger movement of many groups known as the "migration of peoples." As the Slavs settled in their new homelands, they gradually assimilated many of the different peoples already living in those areas.

New Arrivals and New States

The second period, from about the ninth to about the fourteenth centuries, began with the arrival of the Hungarians. Their control of the Hungarian Plain divided the Slavs into their southern and eastern branches. By the year 1000, German colonists were moving eastward into various parts of Eastern Europe. Certain areas such as the Sudeten Mountains and East Prussia became largely Germanized, as did many cities and towns in other areas. Jews from German areas also were moving eastward into the region, where they often established their own settlements.

This period witnessed the rise and decline of states organized by the Poles, Czechs, and Hungarians in the central and northern parts of Eastern Europe. Farther south, the Bulgarians, the Croats, and the Serbs all established states in the Balkan Peninsula. The Croats were conquered by the Hungarians in the twelfth century, while the Bulgarians and Serbs eventually were overwhelmed by the expanding Ottoman Empire in the late fourteenth century.

The Age of Empires

Eastern Europe now entered a third era, during which foreign empires consolidated control over the region and its people. The Ottoman Turks, who come from Asia Minor, were the first outsiders to establish a foothold. They broke into the Balkans

in the fourteenth century and by the sixteenth century controlled most of the peninsula. They also had defeated the Hungarians and occupied most of their territory. Only tiny
Montenegro, a mountainous stronghold near the Adriatic coast,
remained free of Turkish control. While the Turks, who were
Muslims, did not try to convert their Christian subjects in the
Balkans, they deprived the Christians of all political rights,
made them legal inferiors, and taxed them mercilessly. More
dreaded and hated than any money tax was the so-called blood
tax—the periodic taking of Christian boys between the ages of
five and twelve from their parents. These boys were raised as
Muslims in the Ottoman capital of Constantinople and trained
to serve in the empire's elite fighting force, the Janissaries.

The Turks controlled Hungary for about 170 years. Despite
many revolts, their control over the Balkans lasted for 500 years.
There were many negative legacies of the long period of Turkish rule in the Balkans, including a tradition of corrupt government. However, the worst legacy was that Turkish rule cut off
the Balkans from the mainstream of European life. While
Europe was making enormous intellectual, scientific, and economic progress, the Ottoman Empire during that era entered a
period of stagnation, dragging the people of the Balkans down
with it and creating a gap between them and their neighbors to
the west that has not been overcome to this day.

The process of pushing the Turks back did not begin until
late in the seventeenth century. That effort fostered the territorial growth of the region's second foreign master, the Hapsburg Empire. The core of this empire, which was ruled by a
German dynasty, was in Austria. Its status as one of Europe's
great powers really dated from 1683, when, with Polish help,
it beat back the Turks in their siege of Vienna. By 1699 Hapsburg armies had driven the Turks from Hungary. During the
next forty years the Hapsburgs drove the Turks from northern
Serbia and small sections of the northern Balkan Peninsula,
but they did not advance farther until late in the nineteenth
century. Meanwhile, a third foreign power, the Russian

Empire, had pushed into the region from the east. By the eighteenth century, Poland's power was fading rapidly. Between 1772 and 1795 it was partitioned three times. Russia got the largest share while two German states, the Hapsburg Empire and the increasingly powerful Kingdom of Prussia, received smaller ones.

The partition of Poland meant that by the late eighteenth century Prussia (after 1871 called the German Empire) had become a fourth empire with territory in Eastern Europe. The Prussian/German empire in a sense was yet another foreign power that had seized a part of the region. Most of its territory lay farther west, especially after the unification of Germany in 1871. At the same time, however, Prussia may be considered part of the region. It had territory in Eastern Europe before the partition of Poland, and ethnic Germans were the majority in most of that territory. This German-populated area included East Prussia and Pomerania along the Baltic coast and Silesia, an inland region northeast of Bohemia.

Revolution and Nationalism

The fourth period of Eastern European history began with the French Revolution of 1789. The spread of French revolutionary ideas encouraged nationalist feelings and a revived struggle by the subject peoples of the region to retain their national identities and reestablish their political independence. By the mid-nineteenth century the Austrian Empire faced nationalist pressures from many of its non-German subjects, including the Romanians, Czechs, Croats, Slovenes, Slovaks, Serbs, and Hungarians. In 1867 the monarchy was reorganized. In place of the old Austrian Empire, the reforms created the "dual monarchy" of Austria-Hungary. Its Austrian and Hungarian halves were united by the same Hapsburg ruler, who governed as both the emperor of Austria and the king of Hungary. For the most part, however, the Hungarians controlled their part of the empire. These reforms satisfied the Hungarians, but left the empire's subject Slavs increasingly restive. To the north, Russian control over Poland remained intact despite Polish revolts in 1830 and 1863.

The Ottoman Empire was less able to cope with its problems. It lagged behind Europe technologically and was weakened by internal corruption. During the nineteenth century, battlefield defeats at the hands of Russia and Austria-Hungary and revolts by its subject peoples loosened and virtually broke its grip on the Balkans. By the end of the 1870s the Ottoman Empire, by now known as the "sick man of Europe," had lost Bosnia-Herzegovena to Austria-Hungary. It also was forced to grant independence to Montenegro, Serbia, and Romania and autonomy to Bulgaria.

In 1912, Greece (independent since 1829), Montenegro, Serbia, and Bulgaria (independent since 1908) attacked the Ottomans and seized almost all their European territory. A new state, Albania, now achieved independence. The Ottomans retained only the corner of the Balkan Peninsula around Constantinople. The Ottoman defeat, however, did not bring peace; a dispute over the spoils led to a second Balkan war in 1913. A year later, the long-simmering friction between Serbia and Austria-Hungary over Bosnia-Herzegovena produced the deadly spark that ignited World War I.

The Interwar Years and World War II

The fifth period of Eastern European history dates from the end of World War I in 1918 to the end of World War II in 1945. World War I ended with the dissolution of both the Austrian and Ottoman empires. The Russian Empire also collapsed, but was replaced by the Soviet Union. The Soviets, however, lost control of Russia's Polish territory. The overall result was a new look for Eastern Europe. A newly independent Poland, whose boundaries included territory taken from Germany, Russia, and the defunct Austria-Hungary, shared the northern part of the region with Germany. Just to the south was the newly created country of Czechoslovakia and an independent Hungary. In the Balkans,

Serbia, Montenegro, and several other south Slavic regions were stitched together into the new state of Yugoslavia. Romania, Bulgaria, and Albania were still independent.

During the brief period of peace between the two world wars many Eastern European countries had territorial claims against each other. Several also feared claims on their territory by Germany or the Soviet Union. The new borders also left many countries with ethnic minorities who often were subject to discrimination. The Great Depression, which began in 1929 and dragged on through the 1930s, increased economic hardship in a region already plagued by economic problems. Of all the countries in Eastern Europe, only Czechoslovakia managed to achieve a reasonable degree of economic prosperity and remain a democracy. Unfortunately, these achievements were not enough to save it. In 1938 Nazi Germany plunged all of Europe into the dreadful nightmare of World War II. For most of the war, Germany and local governments allied with it controlled Eastern Europe.

The Communist Era

The end of World War II marked the beginning of the sixth period of Eastern European history—Communism and control by the Soviet Union. Communism came to Eastern Europe after the Soviet army drove the Germans out. After Germany surrendered, the Soviets kept their troops in Eastern Europe and used that leverage to put Communist dictatorships in power. This process took varying amounts of time, depending on the country involved. A Communist puppet regime under Moscow's control was running Poland by early 1945, while it took until 1948 for Communists to seize control of Czechoslovakia. Only in Yugoslavia and Albania did local Communist parties come to power largely on their own. In both countries, the Communists had fought guerrilla wars against the Germans during World War II. After the war they used their military forces to seize power and eliminate all political opponents. In the West, people referred to the Communist countries of Eastern Europe as Soviet satellites, meaning that although in theory they were independent, in reality they were under Moscow's control.

There were three main phases to Communist rule in Eastern Europe. Under the leadership of the Soviet Union's brutal dictator, Joseph Stalin, there were forced industrialization (in which the state took control of all industry), collectivization (under which the state forced farmers to give up their land and work on large state-controlled farms), and terror (mass arrests and executions).

Even during the harsh Stalin era, the Soviet Union had trouble maintaining its control over Eastern Europe. In 1948, a series of disputes between Stalin and Josip Broz Tito, the leader of Yugoslavia, led to a split in the Communist world. Yugoslavia remained Communist, but broke free from Moscow's control and took a neutral position in the Cold War between the Western democracies and the Soviet Union. After Stalin's death, in 1953, the problem became worse. The new Soviet leaders were determined to maintain Communist dictatorships. However, they also wanted to rule without resorting to Stalin's brutal methods and to raise the low standard of living in the Communist world. They therefore introduced limited political and economic reforms. Stalin's death and the reforms that followed encouraged the people of Eastern Europe; they became impatient for greater change and less afraid to defy their Communist rulers. This made it much more difficult for the Soviet Union to keep its satellites in line.

The death of Stalin began the second phase of Soviet control of Eastern Europe, which lasted until 1985. Although the presence of Soviet troops usually kept the lid on during this period, beginning with the 1950s a number of crises erupted in the region. In the spring of 1953, workers in Czechoslvakia struck and rioted against harsh government economic policies. The police cruelly suppressed these protests. In June, a huge protest and riot rocked East Berlin, the capital of East Germany. This time local police could not control the situation. The Soviet Union responded by using tanks and brutal force to crush the uprising.

As part of its program to consolidate control over Eastern Europe, in 1955 the Soviet Union organized its satellites into a military alliance called the Warsaw Pact, which it dominated. In February 1956, however, the new Soviet leader, Nikita Khrushchev, set the stage for more trouble when he denounced Stalin as a brutal dictator in a "secret speech" to the 20th Congress of the Soviet Communist Party. Khrushchev made the speech, which almost immediately became widely known, because he wanted to introduce limited reforms at home. His main goals were to end Stalin's system of terror and raise the Soviet standard of living. These reforms were intended to strengthen the Soviet system, not change it in any fundamental way. Still, the "secret speech" fanned the hopes for real change in Eastern Europe, especially in Poland and Hungary.

By the autumn of 1956 tensions reached the crisis stage in both countries. The Soviets defused the crisis in Poland by making concessions that allowed Polish leaders some autonomy in local matters. However, in Hungary the anger against the Soviet Union turned into a full-fledged revolt. Soviet troops and tanks crushed the revolt, killing thousands of Hungarians in the process. In 1961, there was trouble again in East Germany. This time the Soviet Union and the East German government built the Berlin Wall to stop the thousands of East Germans, mostly young people, who every week were fleeing Communism by crossing over into West Berlin. In 1968, the Soviet Union sent troops to Czechoslovakia to overthrow a local group of Communist leaders who had introduced democratic reforms that Moscow feared might undermine its control of the entire region.

In the end force and intimidation could not make the people of Eastern Europe accept Communism or Soviet control of their countries. Defiance of the Soviet Union was especially

East and West German soldiers guard one
of the first openings in the Berlin Wall in 1989.

visible in Poland. In 1970, protesting workers forced the Communist Party to install a new leader. In 1980, Polish workers were able to organize an independent trade union called Solidarity. It was the first trade union free of government control in any Communist country. In December 1981, Poland's government, under intense Soviet pressure, arrested Solidarity's leaders, disbanded the union, and declared martial law.

This victory turned out to be short-lived. In 1985, the Soviet Union began its own reforms under its new leader, Mikhail Gorbachev. This marked the start of the third, and final, phase of Soviet control of Eastern Europe. As Gorbachev's reforms became more radical over the next few years, they increasingly undermined the Communist regimes of Eastern Europe. By 1989, those regimes, once supported by the steel of the Soviet Army, were resting on hollow and crumbling foundations.

1989: The Year of the People

In 1989, over a period of only a few months, the Communist governments of Eastern Europe collapsed one by one. The chain reaction that broke Communist control of Eastern Europe began in Poland.

In April, the Communist government, desperate to gain public support, legalized Solidarity. It also agreed to parliamentary elections in which non-Communists could run for office. These would be the first free elections in Eastern Europe in four decades. Two months later Solidarity-backed candidates swept to an overwhelming victory. In August, a new government with non-Communists in control took power in Poland. It was the first such government anywhere in Eastern Europe since 1948.

By the spring of 1989 Communism also was collapsing in Hungary. In May, the government punched a hole in the Iron Curtain when it removed the barbed-wire fence separating Hungary from Austria. At the beginning of October, the Hungarian Communist Party dissolved itself and Communist rule in effect came to an end.

In East Germany, the Communist Party put up a stiffer fight, but to no avail. By the summer, thousands of East Germans were fleeing the country by crossing the border into Hungary. Hundreds of thousands more were demonstrating in the streets of several East German cities. Police armed with riot sticks and water cannon could not stop the demonstrations. Nor did it help when the Communist Party changed its leadership. On November 9, the most dramatic event of a dramatic year took place when the East German government tore down the Berlin Wall. Suddenly, the most important physical symbol of the Cold War was transformed from a grim reminder of international tensions to a place of celebration. But not even that step could save the regime. By the end of the year Communism in East Germany was dead.

The Communist government in Czechoslovakia held on a little longer. In mid-November police brutally beat protesters in Prague, the country's capital. By December the Communist regime had collapsed. A new cabinet formed in mid-December gave Czechoslovakia its first government with a non-Communist majority since the Communist seizure of power in February 1948.

Meanwhile, the Communist regime in Bulgaria removed its old hard-line leaders. The new party leaders continued to govern, but had to agree to free elections in early 1990. The only serious violence that marred these remarkable events occurred in Romania, where it took several days of bloody fighting to topple that county's corrupt and brutal regime. As 1989, the Year of the People, came to an end, Communism and Soviet control had been swept from Eastern Europe. Communists officially still controlled Yugoslavia, but in name only. Yugoslavia was on the verge of disintegration, and by early 1990 non-Communists controlled several parts of the country. Only in Albania, which had broken with the Soviet Union in 1961, did a functioning Communist government survive the Year of the People. That regime lasted less than two more years before losing power in 1991.

The year 1989, therefore, was the beginning of the seventh period in the history of Eastern Europe: the era of genuine independence. This era has the potential to mark a fundamental break with the past. For centuries Eastern Europe was a model of what geographers call a "shatter belt": a small band of states dominated by outside powers. The crucial question for these states was whether they were permanently doomed to be the pawns of powerful outsiders, or whether they could establish genuine independence. During the 1990s, having finally emerged from the shadow of Soviet control, the dozen countries of Eastern Europe were able to make their own decisions to a degree unprecedented in their histories. They waited a long time for that opportunity.

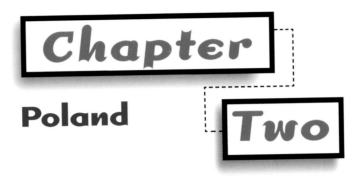

Chapter Two

Poland

Poland, Europe's eighth-largest country, is by far the largest and most populous country in Eastern Europe. Only Romania is even two-thirds as large; of the other ten countries in the region, only Bulgaria has a third as much territory as Poland. Romania has slightly more than half of Poland's population; no other Eastern European country has as much as a third.

Tribes probably first settled parts of what today is Poland as early as the fifth or sixth century, although some estimates place them there even earlier. One of those tribes, the Polanie, or "people of the plain," settled in the territory that today forms the heart of Poland and eventually gave the country its name. However, the Poles' early arrival did not bring them peace; they had settled a land without natural boundaries, exposed to outside invaders. The earliest pressure came from Germans pushing into Polish-inhabited territory from the west and nomadic hordes invading Europe from the east. The German pressure remained a constant in Polish history. Nomadic pressure from the east ended after the fourteenth century, when the last Asian horsemen faded from the scene. But by the seventeenth century a new power, Russia, was strong enough to threaten Poland on its eastern flank. Poland and Russia became bitter rivals, which left Poland in great danger as its power gradually eroded.

Poland's weakness cost it dearly. In the late eighteenth century it was divided between Russia, Prussia, and Austria. Its reemergence as an independent state in 1918 did not solve its security problems, for by the 1930s Poland was squeezed between Europe's two totalitarian powers: Nazi German and Soviet Russia. The result was another half century of foreign oppression—five years of murderous Nazi occupation during World War II followed by more than four decades of Soviet domination during the Cold War.

During the millennium since its emergence as an independent state in the tenth century, Poland's boundaries have changed many times. From its original territory along the Vistula River Poland expanded and shrank, and shifted eastward and westward, as its power, and that of its neighbors, grew or ebbed. At one point in its history, Poland was the largest state in all of Europe. At another, from 1795 to 1918, an independent Poland did not exist at all. Ironically, when the Soviet Union redrew its boundaries after World War II, Poland was almost exactly where it had been when it began its history as an independent state a thousand years earlier.

Geography and People

Poland occupies a squarish chunk of land on the North European Plain. With an area of about 120,500 square miles (312,000 square kilometers), it is slightly smaller than New Mexico. The country is mainly a flat plain, except in the south where its border is formed by the Sudeten Mountains in the west, the Tatra Mountains in the center, and the Carpathians in the east.

Moving from north to south, Poland is made up of five geographic belts. The northwestern sliver of the country along the bays and lagoons of the Baltic Sea gives Poland a coastline about 310 miles (500 kilometers) long. Immediately to the south of the coastal region is a range of hills called the Baltic Heights. They reach the southeastern shore of the Baltic coast near the port city of Gdansk. These two regions are dotted by thousands of lakes that date from the end of the last ice age. The largest of these gifts from a vanished Scandinavian glacier are the Great Masurian Lakes in the northeastern part of the country, which the Poles call the "land of a thousand lakes." They are sparkling jewels in a beautiful region of forests and rolling hills whose winding shoreline is broken by countless inlets, peninsulas, and small islands. Poland has more of these glacial lakes than any European country except Finland. The largest is Lake Sniardwy.

Poland's richest farmland lies in its third belt, a broad plain that covers the central third of the country. Warsaw, Poland's capital and largest city, is in this region. A fourth belt, covering most of southwestern Poland, consists of two upland regions divided by the valley of the Vistula River. One, west of the Vistula in an area called Little Poland, is the Silesian Plateau. The other, rising to the east, is the Lublin Hills. Poland's fifth geographic region is its southernmost territory. Here the country's highest mountains form a barrier separating Poland from its southern neighbors. The Tatra Mountains, which really are part of the Carpathians, have Poland's highest peak, Mount Rysy (8,200 feet, or 2,499 meters).

The Vistula River, more than 620 miles (998 kilometers) in length, is Poland's longest and most important river. It rises in the Carpathians in the far south and then flows northward in an S-shaped course through the heart of the country before emptying into the Baltic Sea in the Gulf of Danzig. The Vistula also flows through the heart of Polish history. It was along its banks that the Polish people emerged as an identifiable group. Today, about midway on the Vistula's course to the sea, Warsaw stands along its banks. Poland's national anthem reflects the Vistula's importance to its people when it proclaims, "We shall cross the Vistula . . . We shall remain Poles."[1]

Other important Polish rivers, all of which flow generally from south to north, include the Bug, the Warta, and the Oder. The Oder, after flowing northeast, turns due north when it meets the Neisse River. From that point on until it reaches the Baltic Sea it marks Poland's boundary with Germany.

Poland was once covered by dense forests. Today about one-fourth of the country remains forest. Successive governments have continued the effort to preserve that important natural resource. In some regions a smattering of the original primeval forests remain, especially in the Bialowieza National Park in the eastern part of the county along the border with Belarus. The Bialowieza park also is home to Europe's last remaining bison, an animal that once roamed much of the continent. The bison is one of Poland's ninety species of mammals. Among Poland's hundreds of species of birds is the white eagle, its national bird.

Poland's main natural resources are coal, copper, sulfur, natural gas, lead, and salt. Its agricultural sector produces grains, hogs, dairy products, potatoes, sugar beets, and oilseed. The country's industries produce machines, iron and steel, ships, automobiles, chemicals, textiles and clothing, processed foods, glass, and beverages.

About 38.7 million people live in Poland. Before World War II Poland was home to several large minority groups, including 4.5 million Ukrainians, 3.3 million Jews, 1 million Belarusians, and 800,000 Germans. The horrors of the war and its chaotic aftermath drastically changed the country's ethnic makeup. Nazi Germany murdered more than 90 percent of Poland's Jews in the Holocaust; after the war most surviving Jews emigrated. Postwar border changes placed most of Poland's Ukrainians and Belarusians in the Soviet Union. Most Germans were expelled or emigrated. Today ethnic Poles make up 98 percent of the country's population. The largest remaining minority groups are Ukrainians and Belarusians, although there are smaller communities of Slovaks, Lithuanians, and Germans. Only about 3,000 Jews still live in Poland.

Between 5 and 10 million people of Polish descent live outside Poland. The largest overseas Polish community is in the United States. Poles occasionally joke that the world's second-largest Polish city is Chicago, home to almost a million people who trace their ethnic roots to Poland.

Poland was a predominantly rural country well into the twentieth century. Today over 60 percent of the population live in cities. The largest cities, aside from Warsaw, are Lodz, Cracow, Wroclaw, Poznan, and Gdansk. Two of them have played a special role in Poland's history. Cracow was its capital and cultural center for more than five hundred years. Gdansk, long a part of Germany and a largely German-populated port city until after World War II, in 1980 was the birthplace of the Solidarity labor union. This in effect made Gdansk the city in which Poland's postwar freedom was reborn.

Poland and the Catholic Church

Virtually all ethnic Poles follow the Roman Catholic faith. Christianity came to Poland in the tenth century when its first ruler, Prince Mieszko, had himself baptized. Mieszko's choice of the Catholic Church based in Rome, instead of the Orthodox Church based in Constantinople, was fateful, for it tied Poland's cultural development to Western Europe rather than to the eastern, and Orthodox, part of the continent. Still, it took time and pressure before the pagan Slavic tribes gave up their traditional religion, but by the twelfth century most Poles were Catholics.

The Catholic Church played an increasingly important role in Polish life. When Poland lost its independence in the eighteenth century, the Church provided a sense of national identity that held Poles together even though they lived under the

The buildings of Jagiellonian University, 650 years old and still a vibrant, important force in education in Poland

rule of three foreign empires. For example, after 1867 public use of the Polish language was forbidden in Austrian-controlled parts of Poland. This left religious devotion as the main form of national self-expression for Poles living under Austrian rule. Catholicism also was a central part of Polish resistance to domination by Russia, the Orthodox giant that controlled most of the Polish heartland for more than a hundred years. The Church played this role again during the Nazi occupation in World War II.

The Church's importance in Polish life, already great, became even more pronounced during the era of Soviet-imposed Communism after 1945. To the Communists, who officially were atheists and regarded all religion as reactionary superstition, the Catholic Church by definition was a dangerous enemy, perhaps the state's most dangerous enemy in Poland. When the Communist regime felt strong enough, it tried to impose restrictions on the Church. These restrictions were particularly severe between 1953 and 1956. Cardinal Stefan Wyszynski, the head of the Polish Church, was held under house arrest. Eight bishops and more than a thousand priests were imprisoned. However, when it was in trouble the Communist regime tried to compromise with the Church to win popular support. After 1970, the Church won increasing rights to carry on its religious and educational activities. By the mid-1970s it was supporting popular resistance to Communist rule that continued until the fall of the Communist regime. Resistance to Communism received a major symbolic boost in 1978, when Cardinal Karol Wojtyla, a Pole from Cracow, became Pope John Paul II. He electrified Poland when he visited there in 1979 and told his countrymen, "Do not be afraid."

Since the fall of Communism, the Catholic Church has tried to expand its influence on Polish life. Ironically, this has hurt rather than helped its popularity. Many Poles, including large numbers of intellectuals and others influenced by the democratic ideals of the West, believe religion should be a private matter. They argue that in a modern democratic society there should be a complete separation between church and state. Many secular Poles and intellectuals have opposed the Church's attempts to promote religious instruction in the public schools and resented its successful campaign to pass a strict law banning abortion. Thus, while just after the fall of Communism 90 percent of all Poles considered the Church the most respected institution in their country, by 1991 that figure had dropped to 58 percent, placing it in second place behind the army.

Polish History to 1945

Poland's history as a state began in 966, when Prince Mieszko had himself and his leading nobles baptized into the Catholic Church. Although Catholicism later would occupy a central place in Poland's spiritual and cultural identity, Mieszko's decision was a political step designed to win recognition for his state from other leaders. The Piast Dynasty that Mieszko founded ruled Poland for the next four centuries. Mieszko's son, Boleslaw the Brave, built on his father's foundations and by 1025 had won recognition as Poland's first king. Boleslaw ruled over a country that was one of the most powerful in the region. His son, Boleslaw the Bold, expanded the boundaries of his kingdom until its borders were very similar to Poland's today.

Despite its successes, Poland constantly was under German pressure. That was the reason for the decision in 1038 to move the country's capital from the western city of Poznan to Cracow in the southeast. However, by 1150 Poland was weakening. In 1241 the Mongols, the fierce and irresistible nomadic conquerors of lands from China to the Middle East to Central Europe, invaded Poland and caused enormous destruction. The Mongols continued their devastating raids for the next fifty years. At the same time, Poland was threatened by a German crusading order called the Teutonic Knights. By 1300, foreigners controlled two thirds of Poland.

Just when Poland's future independence was becoming doubtful, the country began its recovery under the last rulers of the Piast Dynasty. The recovery included the founding of Poland's first university in Cracow in 1364 and reached a new and significant stage shortly after the Piast Dynasty died out. In 1386, Poland's queen married the Grand Duke of Lithuania. Their marriage joined the two neighbors in a confederation, united by their common dynasty. It was, at first, an odd union. Poland was largely Catholic and Lithuania was Europe's last pagan state. It also was a huge state, with territory that extended deep into what today is Ukraine and Belarus. But the two countries were driven together by powerful common enemies, in particular the Teutonic Knights. The new state they formed became the largest in Europe and lasted for four hundred years. Poland gained a new dynasty, the Jagiellons, and Lithuania was converted to a new religion, Catholicism. In

1410, the new union proved its military value when a Polish-Lithuanian force crushed the Teutonic Knights at the Battle of Grunwald (in German, the Battle of Tannenberg).

For the next three centuries Poland was a great power in Europe. It reached a cultural peak in the sixteenth century under the influence of the European Renaissance, which had begun in Italy more than two centuries earlier. The University of Cracow became a world-class center of learning. Its most famous student was Nicholas Copernicus, who in 1543, the year he died, revolutionized astronomy with the publication of *On the Revolutions of the Heavenly Spheres*, in which he argued that the sun, not the earth, was the center of the universe. In Milolej Rej, Poland found its first major author who wrote in everyday language. Renaissance Poland also produced Jan Kochanowski, widely considered the best poet in any Slavic language prior to the nineteenth century.

Poland's glory was not destined to last. Its nobility, or *szlachta*, had enormous powers. They included the right to elect the king, although in practice the Jagiellons functioned as a hereditary dynasty. The nobles also had a parliament, the *Sejm*. However, its rules required unanimous agreement to pass laws. This extreme guarantee of minority rights made it very difficult to govern. In 1569 the Union of Lublin tightened the bonds between Poland and Lithuania, creating what was called the Polish-Lithuanian Commonwealth. But the tighter union did nothing to make the country more governable. When the Jagiellon Dynasty died out in 1572, the nobility's power increased. The *Sejm* affirmed its right to elect Poland's king. This dangerously eroded the power of the central government. It also gave foreign powers the chance to interfere in Poland's affairs every time a king died and a new one had to be elected. And there were powerful and ambitious states on Poland's flanks ready to take advantage of any weakness: Sweden to the north, Russia to the east, the Ottoman Empire to the south, and the Hapsburg Empire to the southwest.

Beginning in 1648, Poland was rocked by a series of disasters that eventually became known as the *potop*, or deluge. It began with a massive revolt in the east by Ukrainian Cossacks. A series of wars followed with Sweden, Russia, and the Ottoman Empire. By the time the smoke of battle cleared, Poland, despite some victories, had lost territory to Russia, Sweden, and Prussia. Poland's population losses were enormous, its cities and towns were devastated, its economy ruined. A last blaze of glory occurred in 1683 when King Jan Sobieski led the Polish cavalry in the dramatic and historic charge that broke the Turkish siege of Vienna. Sobieski's victory ended the Turkish advance into Europe. It set the stage for the more than two-hundred-year European counteroffensive that ultimately drove the Turks from all but a tiny corner of the continent.

Sobieski was hailed as the "Savior of Europe," but neither he nor his successors could save Poland. The country sank into political chaos and slid toward economic bankruptcy. In 1772, Prussia, Russia, and Austria seized large chunks of the country in what is called the first partition of Poland. That event produced a shock that finally brought Poles together to undertake reforms, which culminated in 1791 in Europe's first written constitution. It was based on progressive and democratic ideals and the example of the Constitution adopted by the United States only a few years before. Today, the adoption of the Constitution of May 1791 is marked by an important holiday in Poland. But the constitution had a short life. It was annulled after antidemocratic nobles encouraged Russia to invade Poland. The second partition followed, this time with only Russia and Prussia taking part. The second partition sparked a Polish revolt in 1794, led by Tadeusz Kosciuszko, who had earlier fought for freedom in the American Revolution. The revolt failed, and the next year Russia, Prussia, and Austria carried out the third partition that ended Polish independence.

For more than 120 years the Poles lived under Russian, Prussian, and Austrian rule. The only exception was a brief period from 1808 to 1814 when a semi-independent "Grand Duchy of Warsaw" existed as a puppet of the French emperor Napoleon Bonaparte. Two revolts against Russia, in 1830–1831 and again in 1863, were brutally crushed. Rebellions in 1848 in regions under Prussian and Austrian control were equally unsuccessful.

These defeats did not extinguish Polish national sentiment. The establishment in 1816 of a university in Warsaw reinforced Poland's intellectual ties with Western Europe. Writers and poets, led by Adam Mickiewicz (1798–1855), Poland's greatest poet, often stressed national and patriotic themes. So did Frédéric Chopin (1810–1849), Poland's best-known musician and one of Europe's renowned nineteenth-century composers. Still, not until 1918, after World War I had brought about the collapse of the German and Russian monarchies and the disintegration of the Austrian Empire, did Poland regain its independence.

Poland officially proclaimed its independence on November 9, 1918. Its first president was the nationalist leader Joseph Pilsudski. Poland's interwar history, like that of most of Eastern Europe, was troubled. In 1920 in a short, fierce war with the Soviet Union, Poland won territory inhabited mainly by Ukrainians and Belarusians. Poland also seized the city of Vilnius (in Polish, Wilno) from Lithuania. Its expanded borders created a country in which one third of the population was made up of ethnic minorities. Throughout the interwar period Poland experienced economic problems, most of the rural population remained illiterate, and industry did not grow enough to provide jobs for an expanding population. Yet Poland nonetheless enjoyed a creative intellectual life centered in Warsaw and cities like Vilnius and Lwow. Vilnius was the home of Czeslaw Milosz (1911–), who in 1980 was to win the Nobel Prize for Literature.

World War II again ended Polish independence. In September 1939 it was partitioned between Nazi Germany and the Soviet Union according to an agreement reached by Hitler and Stalin the previous month. The German attack on the Soviet

Union in 1941 put all of Poland under German occupation. While the entire population suffered dreadfully, by far the worst horrors befell Poland's Jewish community. The Nazis murdered 3 million of Poland's 3.3 million Jews. Altogether, 6 million Polish citizens—Christian and Jewish—died during the war.

Germany's defeat in 1945 restored Poland to the map, but with a new set of borders. Poland lost land in the east to the victorious Soviet Union and gained land in the west from a defeated Germany. More important, while Poland was restored to the map, its independence was more a fiction than a fact. Occupied by Soviet troops, Poland faced forty-four years of Soviet domination and Communist rule.

Poland Under Communism, 1945–1989

The period from 1945 until Stalin's death in 1953 was the most oppressive and brutal of the Communist era. The Polish Communist Party (officially the Polish United Workers Party) ruled the country as a puppet of Moscow. All dissenting political groups were silenced, their leaders imprisoned or forced to leave the country. Thousands of people from all walks of life were arrested, the wave of terror reaching its peak in the early 1950s. The Polish economy was restructured on the Communist model; all economic life, including all industries and farms, was placed under state control. A huge army of more than 400,000 troops was organized under Soviet command. The Catholic Church was a major target of persecution.

Still, the Polish people never accepted Communism or Soviet domination. After Stalin's death, his successors in Moscow ended his terroristic methods. Poles responded by demanding greater and more meaningful reforms. In 1956, these protests turned into serious riots by students and workers. The Soviets, fearful of pushing too hard and provoking a massive national uprising, made concessions by allowing a reform-minded Communist who had been imprisoned under

Stalin to become Poland's Communist Party leader. The party's reforms included freeing political prisoners, improving relations with the Church, and returning farming to private hands. However, in 1970 continued poor living conditions and food price increases provoked new riots.

In June 1979 millions of Poles came out to see their countryman Pope John Paul II when he visited his homeland. The next year discontent erupted once again, but this time in a way that, it turned out, permanently crippled the Communist Party's ability to govern. The trouble began with a strike at the Lenin Shipyards in the city of Gdansk. The shipyard workers found a remarkable leader in an electrician named Lech Walesa. Going beyond striking, the workers formed an independent labor union they called Solidarity. It was the first union independent of state control in the history of the Communist bloc. It also was illegal according to Polish law. But the Communist regime was too weak to resist the workers' demands, and in August 1980 it legalized the union. Neither Poland nor Eastern Europe would ever be the same.

Solidarity soon had ten million members, more than one out of every four Poles. Its enormous appeal worried Communist leaders everywhere, and the Polish government found itself under increasing Soviet pressure to crack down on the union. It finally did so in December 1981 by declaring martial law and arresting thousands of union members. Martial law remained in effect until July 1983.

From 1981 until 1989, Poland was immobilized. The government had the guns and power, but it faced such widespread passive resistance from the people, strongly backed by the Church, that it could not govern. Meanwhile, after 1985 the Soviet Union began a program of reform under its new leader, Mikhail Gorbachev, who began urging Eastern European leaders to follow his example. By 1988, Poland's Communist regime was beginning to crack. In a desperate attempt to win public support, the government, in April 1989, again legalized Solidarity and agreed to Poland's first reasonably free elections since World War II. The elections were scheduled for June, and the Communists gambled that they could win because Solidarity would have to get organized from scratch and run a campaign in only two months. They lost that gamble, and with it their grip on power.

The Birth of the New Poland, 1989–1995

The April agreement called for elections to choose a new parliament. The newly created upper house with limited powers, the Senate, had 100 seats, and Solidarity was permitted to run candidates for all of them. The lower house, the *Sejm*, was a holdover from the old parliament. It had 460 seats, but Solidarity could run candidates for only 161. Despite having only two months to prepare, Solidarity scored a stunning victory. It won 99 of the 100 Senate seats (the other went to an independent non-Communist) and all 161 *Sejm* seats it was permitted to contest. Communist power swiftly crumbled. In August, the parliament chose newspaper editor and Solidarity official Tadeusz Mazowiecki as Poland's prime minister.

The new government immediately began a series of reforms. Some, mainly involving amendments to the constitution, were relatively easy to accomplish. In December, the parliament changed the country's name from the Communist-era Polish People's Republic to the pre-World War II Polish Republic. It also guaranteed a series of political rights, including equality under the law, to all political parties. That was a fundamental change from the Communist era, when the Communist Party controlled all political life.

Far more difficult to accomplish were economic reforms designed to move from a state-controlled socialist economy to a free-market capitalist economy. A major problem was that despite the problems with the socialist economy—including its inefficiency and widespread corruption that kept the standard of living low for most Poles—it did provide certain protection for the people. Prices were controlled, people were guaranteed jobs, and essentials such as housing, medical care, and basic foods were cheap. Under a free market, prices would rise or fall according to supply and demand, inefficient businesses that could not make a profit would close, and workers would lose their jobs. There were two ways to proceed with the enormous change to a market economy. One possible strategy was to move to a free-market economy gradually while simultaneously trying to protect the people against hardship. The second option was to do the job fast and try to get the country through the painful period of readjustment as quickly as possible.

The government decided on the second, more rapid course, a policy that came to be known as "shock therapy." It called for ending price controls and government subsidies for basic necessities. It also called for "privatization," which meant transferring government controlled industries and businesses to private ownership. Other aspects of shock therapy dealt with currency reform, encouraging exports, holding down wages to limit inflation, and making enterprises still in government hands operate according to profit-and-loss standards.

Shock therapy began in late 1989 and immediately caused great hardship for many ordinary working people. Prices soared; in late 1989 alone, electricity and gas rose by 400 percent, coal by 600 percent. Workers were hurt by a freeze on wages, and some went out on strike in protest. Unemployment, unknown under Communism, reached 25 percent by January 1990 as inefficient industries closed down. Making matters worse, Western Europe and the United States, despite high-sounding verbal support, provided very little financial aid.

Meanwhile, local elections, the first totally free elections in more than fifty years, were held in May. Solidarity candidates did well, but the low voter turnout of only 42 percent was a sign that the people were upset by the hardships of shock therapy. This mood was reflected within Solidarity, where sharp differences of opinion existed. One faction, led by Lech Walesa, favored speeding up economic reform and privatization.

Another group, favoring Prime Minister Mazowiecki, while supporting reform, favored a more gradual approach to end the hardship that was hurting so many people.

In December, Poland held a presidential election. The election was important because the presidency, created in 1989, was the country's most powerful political office. Among the candidates were Walesa and Mazowiecki, who by then had turned from close allies into bitter political opponents. Walesa led in the first round of the elections, but did not receive the required 50 percent of the vote to win election. Mazowiecki trailed badly behind both Walesa and a another candidate, a millionaire Canadian businessman of Polish ancestry. In the second-round runoff, Walesa won the presidency with 74 percent of the vote. As he was sworn into office on December 22, he blinked back tears and told his people, "The bad time, when the authorities of our state were elected under pressure from aliens . . . is coming to an end."[2]

Lech Walesa, for many years an electrician in a shipyard, was overwhelmingly voted in as Poland's president.

The Presidency of Lech Walesa

Walesa's election was a great triumph for him and for Solidarity. Ironically, the triumph deepened the split in Solidarity and further alienated Walesa from much of the organization he had played the leading role in creating. There were two major reasons for discontent with Walesa. Many intellectuals mistrusted him and questioned his fitness for high national office. They questioned his commitment to democracy and feared he might ignore democratic principles in order to implement his policies in the manner of Poland's first president, Joseph Pilsudski, whom Walesa greatly admired. Among these intellectuals was Adam Michnik, a highly respected dissident under the Communist regime, a former Walesa advisor, and the editor of the Solidarity newspaper *Gazeta Wyboircza*. The other reason for discontent was the economic hardship associated with economic reform. By the end of May 1991, Solidarity again was organizing a strike, this time a nationwide general strike directed against . . . Walesa! Farmers also were hurt by Walesa's free-market reforms, which forced them to compete with farmers from Western European countries.

The parliamentary elections of October 1991 reflected the growing discontent. Once again the turnout was low; only 43 percent of the electorate voted. The leading parties were Mazowiecki's Democratic Union and a prosocialist coalition of several groups called the Democratic Left Alliance. Its core was the Social Democratic Party, the successor group to the defunct Communist Party. Each party won about 12 percent of the vote. A series of minor government crises followed in which two prime ministers came and went.

In June 1992, President Walesa finally nominated a prime minister prepared to carry out his program. The new government strongly pushed free-market reforms and immediately faced a monthlong strike by 40,000 copper workers. This was followed in December by an even more serious strike by coal miners protesting reorganization plans that included cutting the number of miners by half. December, however, was marked by a step forward politically with the adoption of the so-called Little Constitution. This was a temporary document designed to bridge the gap between the outmoded 1952 Communist constitution and an unfinished new constitution. There also was a change in the electoral law that required a 5 percent minimum for a party to win representation in the *Sejm*. This was designed to eliminate small parties and thereby improve the chances of forming a stable government.

The fall of 1993 was a memorable one for the Polish people. In October, the last of the Soviet/Russian combat troops that had occupied their country since 1945 finally returned home. That same month Poland again voted for a new parliament. This time the Left Democratic Alliance won a solid victory. It favored a slower pace of reform and a greater emphasis on social programs to help people hurt by economic change. The new prime minister immediately slowed the pace of economic reform, a policy that caused enormous tension with President Walesa. During 1994, as Walesa fought with the prime minister, Solidarity returned to organizing demonstrations and strikes. In February, 20,000 Solidarity demonstrators in Warsaw demanded more government efforts to fight unemployment and help ordinary people; in March a nationwide series of strikes began. In early 1995 tension reached the point where the *Sejm* threatened to impeach Walesa. By May the tension had exploded into violence on the streets of Warsaw, when thirty Solidarity demonstrators were injured during a 10,000-person demonstration to protest rising unemployment and environmental pollution.

Ironically, despite all these troubles, by 1994 the Polish economy had turned the corner and begun to grow. The country's gross domestic product grew by more than 5 percent in 1994 and by 7 percent in 1995. However, these increases were unevenly felt. In particular, the industrial working class, Walesa's core group of supporters, were among the hardest hit between 1990 and 1994 and, as their strike activity indicated, still not benefiting from the free-market reforms by 1995.

The stage was thus set for a showdown between Walesa and the leader of the Left Democratic Alliance, Aleksander Kwasniewski, a forty-year-old, smooth-talking former Communist. It came in the presidential election of November 1995. Walesa, who had risen to fame and power as an ordinary working man, had several disadvantages in the campaign. The problems of economic reform decreased his popularity. Voters also resented his new lifestyle—he had moved from his original presidential home, a reasonably modest dwelling, to a luxurious and newly renovated seventeenth-century palace. Perhaps anticipating hard times ahead, Walesa had his new presidential palace fitted with bullet-proof windows. Walesa's campaigning style also hurt. He called his opponent a liar and a thug. Nor did the support of the Catholic Church help, largely because of its strident attacks on Kwasniewski. Walesa probably was also hurt by his support for the Church's uncompromising opposition to abortion. While most Poles thought abortion was wrong, they believed women had a right to choose when it came to that difficult decision.

Kwasniewski, by contrast, presented a sophisticated, moderate image. While cautiously supporting economic reform, he also stressed the necessity of helping ordinary people get through the hard times. He called himself a "social democrat" and promised he would never take Poland back to Communism. This helped him overcome the revelation that he did not have a university degree, as he had once claimed.

Once again, no candidate won 50 percent of the vote in the first round, although Kwasniewski led Walesa by two percentage points. In the second round, only six years after the fall of Communism, the former Communist won Poland's presidency over the former dissident with 51.7 percent of the vote. Kwasniewski officially took office on December 23, 1995.

From Presidential to Parliamentary Elections, 1995-1997

Kwasniewski began his presidency by trying to bring his increasingly divided country together. He made an attempt to patch up relations with the Catholic Church. However, those relations went from bad to worse over the issue of abortion. In 1993, after an intense campaign by the Church, Poland had adopted one of the world's most restrictive abortion laws. It was permitted only in cases of rape, incest, and a few other conditions. Walesa vetoed an attempt to liberalize the law in 1994. In August 1996, in the face of fierce opposition from the Church and conservative groups, the law was liberalized to allow women with financial or personal problems to end their pregnancies.

The year 1997 began with one of the most ironic events of Poland's post-Communist era. In March, as icy winds blew in from the Baltic Sea, the government announced that the Gdansk shipyard, bankrupt and $134 million in debt, would be closed. It was really a double irony. The Lenin shipyard in Gdansk was founded in 1947 as a showcase of Communist economic development. In 1980 it was the birthplace of Solidarity and of Lech Walesa's political career. Between 1989 and 1994 the shipyard, which was 60 percent government owned and 40 percent worker owned, proved unable to compete in a free-market economy. In other words, it became a victim of Walesa's own economic reforms. Now, in 1997, it fell to a former Communist to close down what was not only a symbol of Solidarity, but also a former Communist showcase. The closing was a terrible blow to Solidarity and to millions of Polish workers. As one shipyard worker said bitterly, "We were not fighting in 1970 and 1980 for a Poland like this. We were fighting for a just Poland for all Poles."[3]

Despite that disappointment, Poland in April took a major political step forward when, after four years of debate and negotiation, it adopted a new constitution. The new constitu-

In 1995 these kids helped out with an Adidas sneaker promotion in the main square of Cracow.

tion slightly weakened the power of the president versus both the *Sejm* and the prime minister. It made it easier for the *Sejm* to override a presidential veto by lowering the percentage of votes needed from two thirds to three fifths and gave the prime minister more control over choosing cabinet ministers.

The year 1997 also brought many Poles something they desperately wanted: an invitation to join the North Atlantic Treaty Organization (NATO). Despite the fall of the Soviet Union, most of the countries of Eastern Europe wanted to join NATO because they still feared Russia and wanted the protection the alliance would bring. The Russians, on the other hand, bitterly opposed NATO's expansion eastward. After long negotiations and delays, NATO in July invited Poland, Hungary, and the Czech Republic to begin negotiations that would lead to membership. There was, of course, an irony here as well, for it was Kwasniewski, before 1989 a Communist and supporter of the Soviet Union, who led his country into NATO.

Kwasniewski's triumph with NATO helped his personal popularity, but it did not do the same for the Democratic Left Alliance as a whole. By the time of the scheduled 1997 parliamentary elections, many Polish voters remained uneasy about the past of the former Communists who made up the Democratic Left Alliance as well as the organization's growing arrogance since taking power. As one middle-aged Warsaw woman put it, "I'm old enough to remember what they were like. And they want to appoint all their people to top posts."[4]

Solidarity was able to take advantage of the situation in part because of Marian Krzaklewski, a computer scientist who became its leader after Walesa's election to the presidency. Krzaklewski was a skilled coalition builder. He gathered more than thirty small political parties and union groupings into a new party called the Solidarity Election Alliance. In September, it swept to victory, winning 201 of the 460 seats in the *Sejm*. The Solidarity Alliance then formed a coalition with the pro–free-market Freedom Union (60 seats) to create a majority in the *Sejm* and form a new government. Poland's new prime minister was Jerzy Buzek, a fifty-seven-year-old chemistry professor known for his sound grasp of economic issues. Buzek was Protestant in overwhelmingly Catholic Poland. The country's new foreign minister, Bronislaw Geremek, a historian and specialist on medieval France, was one of its few remaining Jews.

In the Year 2000

Whatever its lingering problems, by the last years of the 1990s Poland was very different from the country that entered the decade just free from the shadow of Communism. To be sure, the country still had many problems. Although manufacturing as a whole was recovering—it grew by 12 percent in 1995 alone—the mining industry, especially coal mining, was in crisis. The mines remained inefficient and were losing money.

Employment in the mines was expected to drop by 80,000 over the next several years. This was a bitter blow to the miners, who under Communism were the top rung of the working class, with wages five times those of other workers. The mines still operating were adding to the country's already severe environmental problems.

There also was trouble on the farms, where in 1999, 20 percent of all Poles still earned their livelihood. Polish farmers, who generally operated inefficient farms of less than 50 acres (20 hectares), were struggling to compete with cheap food imported from Western Europe. Simply put, Poland's new capitalist economy was not benefiting everyone. Ten years after the fall of Communism more than 10 percent of the country's workers were unemployed.

Poland also remained deeply divided over a number of issues, including abortion. In December 1997, only a few months after taking power, the new Solidarity government passed a new, tough anti-abortion law. The law allowed an abortion only if the mother's life was in danger, if the fetus was severely damaged, or if the pregnancy had resulted from rape. Doctors who performed other abortions faced up to two years in jail.

At the same time, there was a lot on the positive side of the ledger. Poland's presidential elections of 1990 and 1995, and its parliamentary elections of 1993 and 1997, and the peaceful shifts in power they produced, were signs that democracy indeed was taking hold. The economy meanwhile was continuing to grow; in 1997 the growth rate was 6.9 percent, the third consecutive year it exceeded 6 percent. Unemployment, while still at a high 12 percent, was declining. Inflation, which stood at 19 percent in 1996, fell to 13 percent. The shops were full. Progress continued moving the economy from a state-controlled to a free-market system. By 1996, almost four thousand government-owned enterprises had been transferred to private hands. This was done in part by giving workers shares when the enterprises where they worked were privatized and by giving vouchers to 27 million adults. The vouchers could then be invested in privatized companies of their choice or exchanged for shares in fifteen investment funds managing five hundred enterprises.

By the end of 1997 almost two thirds of the economy was in private hands. The hope was that selling off many of the 3,500 remaining state-owed enterprises would raise that figure to 80 percent by 2002. Furthermore, foreign corporations were investing in Poland and introducing modern technology in the process. Between 1989 and the end of 1997, foreigners invested $20 billion in Poland. One of the most important projects was a General Motors automobile plant. Poland also had a modern stock market and banking system, both of which the government set up in the early 1990s.

Even some of Poland's problems were signs of economic progress. By 1997 traffic jams were common in Poland's major cities. In 1995 Poles bought about 255,000 cars. That figure jumped to 374,000 in 1996 and 460,000 in 1997. Traffic accidents, especially those caused by drunk driving, were becoming a national concern. So was the fact that the country had only one major highway. Plans called for a national highway system to be built at a cost of $8 billion. All in all, most Poles probably agreed with a shopper who on the eve of the 1997 parliamentary elections commented that she preferred to focus on the future rather than on the past. "We have to go forward," she said.[5]

No step was more important to millions of Poles than when their country, along with Hungary and the Czech Republic, officially joined NATO. That historic event took place on March 12, 1999, at a ceremony held in the United States. In Warsaw, the celebrations included a fireworks display. As one seventy-five-year-old soldier, who had seen his country suffer at German hands during World War II and at Soviet hands after the war, watched he summed up the national feeling:

> Now we stand a chance as a nation. We stand a chance not to be taken into captivity, to be imprisoned or threatened, so we can live in human dignity in a free country that has earned its freedom.[6]

Chapter

Hungary Three

The Hungarians, or Magyars, in several respects are different from any of their neighbors. They were the last Eastern European group to settle in the region, arriving in the final years of the ninth century. They also speak an unusual language. Hungarian belongs to the Finno-Ugric language group, which is unrelated to any of the world's major language families, including the Indo-European languages spoken by virtually all Europeans. Among the European nations, only the Finns and the Estonians, who live respectively north and east of the Baltic Sea, speak languages related to Hungarian. (A variety of small tribal peoples scattered across northern Eurasia speak other Finno-Ugric languages.)

Whatever the differences between the Hungarians, their Eastern European neighbors, the people of Poland nonetheless have a saying that "Poles and Magyars are two cousins."[1] What the Poles mean is that both peoples have risked spectacular, if often hopeless, battles and uprisings against powerful enemies or rulers. In 1526 a small Hungarian force of 20,000 courageously met the huge invading 100,000-man Turkish army at the Battle of Mohacs, despite having virtually no chance of victory. Hungarians joined in the great revolutionary upheaval that swept much of Europe during 1848 and 1849 in a futile attempt to restore their lost independence. During the Cold War there were violent protests and riots against Soviet control in several Eastern European countries, including Poland. But only the Hungarians, in 1956, mounted an all-out uprising to throw the Soviets out, a desperate effort the Soviets crushed with the use of overwhelming force.

Over the course of their thousand-year history in the region, the Hungarian people have had their share of victories, and have demonstrated the ability to recover from adversity. After bursting into the center of Europe and occupying the Danube Basin in the last years of the ninth century, Hungarian horsemen raided as far afield as Spain, northern Germany, and southern Italy. The Hungarians later built a powerful medieval state that included what today is Hungary, Slovakia, Croatia, and the region of Transylvania which today is part of Romania. The Hungarian kingdom survived until the sixteenth-century Turkish advance into Europe left the Hungarian lands partitioned between the Ottoman and Hapsburg empires for more than 150 years. Eventually, in 1867, the Hungarian landowning class established a partnership with the Austrian Hapsburgs as corulers of the Austro-Hungarian Empire. In the aftermath of the empire's defeat in World War I, Hungary again became independent, but without most of its traditional territory. Budapest, once a grand imperial center, was now the capital of a small, landlocked country. After fighting on the German side during World War II, Hungary endured more than four decades of Soviet domination before achieving real independence when Moscow's satellite empire collapsed in 1989.

Geography and People

Hungary is a compact country virtually in the center of Eastern Europe with an area of about 35,900 square miles (93,000 square kilometers), about the size of Indiana. Shaped roughly like a ragged and dented trapezoid, it extends about 325 miles (524 kilometers) from east to west and about 155 miles (250 kilometers) from north to south.

Most of Hungary is a low-lying plain less than 656 feet (200 meters) above sea level. Hills and mountains in the north and west cover less than 2 percent of the country. The majority of those mountains actually are little more than high hills. Mount Kekas, northeast of Budapest, at just over 3,325 feet (1,014 meters), is Hungary's highest peak. The majestic Danube River runs through Hungary from north to south for more than 250 miles (400 kilometers), about one eighth of its total length. Just north of Budapest the Danube cuts through the Carpathian Mountains at one of its most scenic points, the Danube Bend.

The Danube Bend, an especially beautiful part of the river in Hungary

To the west of the Danube is a long, slender sliver of water called Lake Balaton. Europe's largest freshwater lake west of the former Soviet Union, Lake Balaton covers an area of 230 square miles (592 square kilometers) but averages only 6.5 to 10 feet (2 to 3 meters) in depth. It is a picturesque lake and a major recreational attraction that through the ages has been the subject of countless poems. Hungarians, perhaps carried away by national pride that makes them see their beautiful lake as larger than life, call Lake Balaton the "Hungarian Sea."

Hungary has three main geographic regions. East of the Danube, covering more than half of the country and bisected by the Tisza River, is the Great Hungarian Plain, or *Alfold* in Hungarian. Although it is hard to imagine today as one views this flat open expanse, millions of years ago a mountain range more than 13,000 feet (4,000 meters) high stood here. Shifts in the earth's crust brought down the mighty mountains and created a basin, which then flooded and became an inland sea. Today's plain, its terrain smoothed by the motion of long-departed waters, emerged when the sea dried up. Part of the plain contains the same fertile black soil also found in Poland, Russia, and Ukraine. Helped by modern farming techniques that reduced the threat of flooding, local farmers now raise a wide variety of crops in the region, including wheat, corn, and sugar beets. The eastern part of the plain is a treeless prairie, similar to the Great Plains of North America, called the *puszta*, where for centuries large herds of cattle and horses grazed. Although today crops have replaced many of the herds that once grazed on the *puszta*, the Hungarian *csikos*, or horse-herder, is still a fixture here, providing displays of artistic horsemanship for tourists and other visitors.

West of the Danube, covering about a third of the country, is Transdanubia. Here the countryside is a mixture of plains and rolling hills. The farmers of Transdanubia produce a variety of crops, including grapes for wines that are popular both in Hungary and other parts of Europe. Transdanubia has important mineral resources, among them rich deposits of bauxite. There also are deposits of copper, iron, manganese, and uranium. During the Cold War, Hungary's uranium was mined under the direct control of the Soviet Union. Small deposits of oil and gas also dot the region.

Hungary's third main region, running along the border with Slovakia, is called the Northern Hills. Hungary's major remaining forests, home to wild boar and deer, cover most of this region's hills and mountains. Mineral resources include rich deposits of iron and coal that have been the basis for local industrial development. Grapes grown in the Northern Hills are used to make Hungary's famous Tokay wine.

Hungary was primarily an agricultural country until the twentieth century. It still produces important crops of wheat, barley, corn, potatoes, grapes, sugar beets, apples, and sunflower seeds. However, agriculture was pushed from center stage after World War II, when the Soviet-dominated Communist regime promoted extensive industrialization. Today less than 7 percent of the labor force works in agriculture. Hungary's most heavily industrialized region is around Budapest, although there are several smaller industrial areas. Major products include steel, chemicals, cement, pharmaceuticals, plastics, transport equipment, and processed foods. Despite industrialization, Hungary remains self-sufficient in food and exports large quantities of agricultural products.

Hungary is basically a homogeneous country of about 10.3 million people. Ethnic Hungarians constitute about 90 percent of the population. Gypsies, at about 3 percent of the population, are the largest of Hungary's minority groups. Hungary's approximately 80,000 Jews are the largest remaining Jewish community in Eastern Europe. Hungary also has smaller populations of Germans, Slovaks, Romanians, and Slovenes. More than 60 percent of Hungary's people are urban dwellers, with almost a fifth of the population living in Budapest. About two thirds of all Hungarians are Roman Catholics; another 20 percent are Calvinists, and 5 percent are Lutherans. About 2 million Hungarians live in Transylvania, a region that formerly belonged to Hungary but is now part of Romania, and about 600,000 Hungarians live in Slovakia. Hungary's concern with the status and rights of these two communities continues to cause tensions with both Romania and Slovakia.

Hungarian History to 1945

The Hungarians began their history as a group of tribes known as the Magyars. The Magyars were hunters and fishermen who wandered the endless plains near the Ural Mountains where Asia and Europe meet. They eventually became excellent horsemen and used their skills to conquer the Danube Basin in 896, and to raid other parts of Europe—from Spain, Germany, and Italy in the west to Constantinople in the east—in the decades that followed. The Magyars' days as feared raiders came to an end in 955, when the Holy Roman emperor Otto I crushed them at the Battle of Augsburg. His decisive victory over the fierce Magyar horsemen was one of the reasons Otto became known as Otto the Great.

By the year 1000, many Magyars had adopted Christianity. That year Stephan I, with the blessing of the pope, was crowned the first king of Hungary. Legend says that Stephan received his crown on Christmas Day. Hungary's conversion to the Roman form of Christianity helped link the country to Western Europe and the Western cultural tradition. Stephan I, who died in 1038, was canonized as a Roman Catholic saint in 1083 and has been Hungary's patron saint ever since.

Stephan and his successors built a powerful medieval state that included Slovakia, Transylvania, and Croatia. Two major events of the thirteenth century influenced that state's development. In 1222 the kingdom's nobles forced the king to issue the Golden Bull, which limited the monarch's powers and granted the nobility certain rights. In 1241, disaster struck when the Mongols, the brutal conquerors of Russia and many other lands, stormed into the Danube Basin. Despite receiving little support from his nobles, King Bela IV (1235–1279) went out to meet them. The Mongols routed Bela's army; over the next year they destroyed Hungary's towns and murdered at least a third of its population. Some of Hungary's earliest literature consist of eye-witness accounts of that dreadful invasion, in particular a chronicle in verse composed in Latin, the language of the Church, called *Planctus destructionis regni Hungariae per Tartaros.*

Yet Hungary recovered. Bela IV and his successors encouraged immigration from the west, and many Germans, Italians, and Jews came to rebuild and repopulate Hungary's towns and contribute their skills to its economic and cultural development. By the fourteenth century, Hungary was being enriched by rich local mines that produced one third of Europe's gold and one fourth of its silver. Its first two universities were founded in the second half of the century, one in the city of Pecs in the south and the other at Buda (later Budapest) in the north. Hungary reached a cultural peak in the fifteenth century under the reign of Matthias Corvinus (1458–1490). Its outstanding literary figure was Janus Pannonius (1434–1472), one of the leading European poets of that era. Although Pannonius wrote in Latin, he is considered Hungary's first great poet.

But there was trouble ahead. By the sixteenth century Hungary had been weakened by a peasant revolt against harsh conditions as well as by political infighting and disunity. And a mighty enemy, the Turkish Ottoman Empire, which the Hungarians already had battled and turned back during the fifteenth century, was advancing again from the east. In 1526, the Turks destroyed the Hungarian army at the Battle of Mohacs. They then occupied most of the country despite heroic Hungarian resistance. Hungary ended up divided between the Ottomans and another rising power, the Austrian Hapsburg Empire. It was then was divided another way by the Protestant Reformation. The Reformation took hold in Hungary after the Battle of Mohacs, most strongly in the Turkish-occupied regions. Today most Hungarian Protestants live in the eastern part of the country, a legacy that dates from the sixteenth century.

Hungary remained split between the Hapsburg and Ottoman empires until the late seventeenth century. Finally, in 1686, Hapsburg armies liberated Budapest and drove the Turks from the rest of country. The Ottoman Empire formally gave up its claims to Hungary in the Treaty of Karlowitz in 1699.

It took a long time for Hungary to recover from the effects of the fighting that finally freed them from the Turks. Large parts of the country were depopulated and most of its medieval buildings destroyed. Between 1703 and 1711 there was an unsuccessful rebellion against Hapsburg rule. However, beginning in the mid-1700s and into the nineteenth century, Hungary prospered and advanced culturally under the Hapsburgs.

New tensions between the Hungarians and the Austrians arose in the second quarter of the nineteenth century. Hungarian nationalism combined with democratic political ideas to increase resistance to Austrian rule. Educated Hungarians placed increased importance on the development of Hungarian language and literature. Resistance turned to revolt in 1848. In February, the French overthrew their monarchy. The revolutionary movement spread across Europe, reaching Hungary in March. Its leaders in Budapest were Louis Kossuth, a brilliant speaker who was the son of a landless nobleman, and the poet Sandor Petofi. In April 1849, Kossuth declared Hungary an independent republic. Hungarian forces proved a match for the Austrians, but found themselves overwhelmed when the Russian Empire, fearing that the revolution might spread eastward, sent a huge army to help the Austrian emperor restore order in Hungary. Petofi died fighting the Russians, while Kossuth fled abroad. He remained in exile the rest of his life; after his death in 1894 his body was brought back to Budapest and buried with honors.

By the time of Kossuth's death the Hungarian nobility had significantly strengthened its power within the empire. In 1866, Austria was defeated by Prussia in a short war, an event that highlighted the empire's growing weakness. This led to a series of reforms, including a compromise in 1867 with the

Hungarians that created the Dual Monarchy of Austria-Hungary. The new arrangement, a victory for Hungary at the time, turned out to be a bad bargain in the long run. When Austria-Hungary collapsed after its defeat along with Germany after World War I, the Hungarians were treated as a defeated enemy rather than as a people subject to the Austrians.

Local turmoil, including the establishment of a short-lived Communist regime in 1919, delayed a final treaty with the Allies until 1920. That agreement, the Treaty of Trianon, stripped Hungary of about two thirds of the territory it had once ruled. Romania, Czechoslovakia, Yugoslavia, and even Austria—itself reduced to a small state—gained at Hungary's expense. Most of the lost territory was inhabited by non-Hungarians. However, the losses included Transylvania, where about 2 million Hungarians lived, a prize the Allies gave to Romania. Another 600,000 Hungarians lived in territory turned over to Czechoslovakia.

For the next quarter century, Hungary was driven by its desire to recover its lost lands. At home a dictatorship established in 1920 by Admiral Miklos Horthy protected the interests of a wealthy minority while ignoring the need for meaningful social reforms, including land reform. The Great Depression that began in 1929 caused a severe drop in the standard of living. By the late 1930s Hungary was cooperating with Nazi Germany, and between 1938 and 1941 it took advantage of Germany's aggression to seize territory from several of its neighbors. Hungary also bought German approval by supporting its anti-Semitic policies and passing its own anti-Semitic laws. In 1941, Hungary entered World War II on the side of Germany.

The war was a disaster for Hungary. When the tide of fighting finally turned against Germany in 1943, Hungary's leaders hoped they would be able to surrender to the Western Allies. Instead, in March 1944, Germany occupied the country. This brought immediate catastrophe to Hungary's Jewish community. By the time the Soviet Red Army reached Hungary in October, the Germans had deported and murdered almost two thirds of Hungary's 725,000 Jews. It took until April 1945 for the Soviets to drive the Germans completely out of Hungary and occupy the entire country. They would stay for more than four decades. Hungary's long ordeal with Communism was about to begin.

Hungary Under Communism, 1945–1989

The Hungarian Communist Party did not officially take control of the country until 1947. However, between 1945 and 1947 the presence of Soviet troops and an Allied Control Commission dominated by its Soviet chairman meant that the Soviet Union was in control. It did not matter that the Communist Party, renamed the Hungarian Workers Party in 1948, decisively lost in the free parliamentary elections of November 1945. Over the next two years, backed by the Soviets, it used tactics to bit by bit eliminate the rights of other political parties. Despite a poor showing in parliamentary elections in August 1947, the Communists took complete control of Hungary that year.

Between 1947 and 1953 Hungary was reorganized on the Soviet model as a one-party dictatorship. The state took over the economy. According to Moscow's instructions, Hungarian Communists followed policies of central planning, collectivization of agriculture, and the development of heavy industry. Stalin's death in 1953 enabled moderates within the party to assert their influence. Although the hard-liner Matyas Rakosi remained party leader, Imre Nagy, an advocate of reform and an opponent of Stalinist-type purges and terror, became prime minister. In 1955, however, Nagy was forced to resign and was replaced by a Rakosi ally.

In the wake of Soviet leader Nikita Khrushchev's Secret Speech to the twentieth Congress of the Soviet Communist Party in February 1956 (see chapter 1), Nagy was dramatically returned to power. On October 23, a huge student-led demonstration broke out in Budapest demanding reforms. When police attacked the demonstrators, they fought back. When the government called out the army, many soldiers turned over their weapons to the demonstrators. Not even the presence of Soviet troops on the streets of Budapest intimidated the demonstrators. On October 25, the Communist Party's ruling Central Committee gave in and named Nagy as prime minister.

Moscow accepted the change, hoping that Nagy would be able to introduce cosmetic reforms that would reduce tensions—while continuing the strict adherence to Soviet policies. They soon were disappointed, for events in Hungary were moving faster than in Poland. Pushed by militant crowds demanding real independence, Nagy announced that Hungary was going to abolish its Communist dictatorship and become a democracy. He also announced that Hungary would leave the Warsaw Pact (see chapter 1 and the Encyclopedia). The Soviets responded on November 4 by sending their tanks into Budapest to crush what had become a full-fledged attempt to end their control of Hungary. Nagy went on the radio to speak to his people and appeal for Western help:

> This is Imre Nagy, Premier, speaking. In the early hours
> of this morning, the Soviet troops launched an attack
> against our capital city with the obvious intention of over-
> throwing the lawful, democratic Hungarian Government.
> Our troops are fighting. The government is in place. I
> inform the people of Hungary and world public opinion
> of this.[2]

The Hungarians resisted courageously, using rifles, rocks, and gasoline-filled bottles against tanks, but Soviet strength was overwhelming. About 2,500 Hungarians died in the bitter fighting that lasted until November 11; 200,000 others fled to the West. Additional thousands were imprisoned. During the next five years, 2,000 more people were executed, among them Nagy and four of his top aides, who were secretly tried and hanged in 1958. Nagy was buried in an unmarked grave near the outskirts of Budapest.

Hungarians fleeing restrictive Soviet policies in 1956 leave their homeland and cross the border into Austria.

Hungary's new Soviet-designated leader was Janos Kadar. He would dominate Hungarian political life for the next three decades. Kadar was, as expected, a loyal Soviet puppet, but he also understood the need to try policies that might win him some acceptance with the people. Beginning in 1968 Hungary took the lead in the Soviet bloc with economic reforms called the "new economic mechanism." The reforms slightly relaxed centralized economic planning and used some economic incentives to encourage greater efficiency. During the 1970s and into the 1980s Kadar's limited reforms enabled Hungary to prosper relative to most of the other Soviet satellites. However, by the late 1980s economic stagnation had set in. Meanwhile, the reforms of Mikhail Gorbachev in the Soviet Union had unleashed new pressure for change in Hungary. In 1987, reformer Karoly Grosz took over as prime minister and introduced new reforms; in 1988 he replaced Kadar as party leader. Grosz now was in a position to speed up reform, but in fact it was a matter of too little too late. Hungarians were fed up with Communism and for the first time since 1956 saw a chance to get rid of it. This time, without having to take up arms, they would be successful.

The Birth of the New Hungary

Between 1987 and 1989 there were several increasingly clear signs that Hungary's Communists were losing their grip on power. In September 1987 a newly formed organization, the Hungarian Democratic Forum, openly called for uncensored debates on national issues. In March 1988 a more radical group, the Network of Free Initiatives, added its voice to the demands for change. On October 23, 1989, despite government attempts to prevent it, the Network sponsored a demonstration commemorating the anniversary of the 1956 Revolution. The next month the Network reorganized itself into an openly political organization, the Alliance of Free Democrats, which insisted that Hungary could not make economic progress under the Communists and called for a Western free-enterprise system. Meanwhile, other political groups were organizing that traced their roots to pre-Communist political parties.

By 1989, Hungary's Communist regime was sliding quickly down the slippery slope. In January the government legalized the right to strike and form non-Communist political parties. It also agreed to allow the reburial of Imre Nagy. In March, 100,000 people demonstrated in Budapest demanding genuine democracy and free elections. In May, the government began tearing down the barbed-wire fence along Hungary's border with Austria. This historic step tore open the first huge hole in the Iron Curtain that had divided Europe since the late 1940s. In June, Imre Nagy and the four men executed with him were given their long-overdue proper funerals. Organized by the Hungarian Democratic Forum, the funeral demonstration brought more than 300,000 people to pay tribute to a national hero and the men who died with him. In the presence of Communist officials, speakers praised Nagy and poured scorn on both the Soviet Union and their Hungarian Communist puppets.

The regime's end came quickly. In October the Hungarian Communist Party (since 1958 officially called the Hungarian Socialist Workers Party) dissolved itself. It then reorganized as the Hungarian Socialist Party, but with only 30,000 members, as opposed to the 700,000 members the Communist Party boasted at its peak. On October 23, the anniversary of the 1956 uprising, the Hungarian People's Republic became the Republic of Hungary. The country's constitution was amended to remove the clause guaranteeing one-party rule. Although Communist Party members still held their government posts pending new elections, Hungary's era as a Communist state was over.

A New Decade and a New Government

Hungary's post-Communist era began with parliamentary elections in the spring of 1990. The parliament, called the National Assembly, had 386 deputies. They were elected according to a mixed system of proportional representation and direct-election single-member constituencies. Of the total, 210 were chosen by proportional representation, with each party winning at least 4 percent of the vote (raised to 5 percent in 1994) receiving seats according to its percentage of the vote. The other 176 deputies were elected from individual districts by majority vote. The Hungarian Democratic Forum, which advocated a gradual shift to a free-market system, was the leading vote getter, winning 43 percent of the vote and 165 of 386 parliamentary seats. The Alliance of Free Democrats, which supported a more rapid transition to the free market, came in second with a total of 92 seats. The former Communists who ran as the Hungarian Socialist Party were swept from power, taking only 11 percent of the popular vote and 33 seats in parliament. The Democratic Forum then combined with two small parties and several independent representatives to form a coalition government. Its leader, Jozsef Antall, a respected politician with no ties to the former regime, became prime minister—Hungary's first non-Communist leader in more than forty years. In August, the parliament chose Hungary's president, who is the official head of state. He was Arpad Goncz, a writer and founding member of the Alliance of Free Democrats who had been imprisoned for six years following the 1956 uprising.

The new government was in a difficult position. While most Hungarians recognized that the transition to a market economy would involve difficulties, they also were impatient to see a rapid improvement in their living conditions. They did not. In order to reduce its huge budget deficit, the government cut the subsidies it provided on many products that Hungarians bought every day. The government also decontrolled most prices, a necessary step to establishing a market economy. The result was a disastrous combination: inflation and unemployment. Decontrolled prices skyrocketed; in January 1990 alone, meat, poultry, flour, and dairy products, and cooking fat rose an average of 32 percent. Overall, the inflation rate reached 25 to 30 percent. Meanwhile, unemployment soared and inefficient factories, stripped of their government subsidies, had to close their doors. Between 1990 and 1993 the economy as a whole declined by 18 percent. By then unemployment was over 12 percent. Not until 1994 did the economy begin to grow. Since 1990 already was a bad year—the economy had been declining during the last three years of Communist rule and a quarter of the population lived below the poverty line—the pressure on the people was even greater.

The reaction was soon in coming. In local elections held during the fall of 1990 the governing coalition suffered a severe setback. An opposition group led by the Alliance of Free Democrats won control of Budapest and many other cities. In rural areas, independent candidates won a majority of the votes. Perhaps the most significant result of the election was the apathy of the voters. In only the second free election after more than four decades of Communist dictatorship, less than 40 percent of the electorate even bothered to vote.

This electoral setback did not prevent the Antall government from making substantial progress toward building a free-market economy. The government encouraged the formation of new private businesses and moved forward in privatizing state-owned enterprises. Hungary was more fortunate than its neighbors when it came to privatization because a start had been made in that direction during the last two years of the old Communist regime. As a result, by 1993 the private sector accounted for half of the Hungarian economy. The government also was successful in attracting foreign investment. Among the outside investors that opened plants in Hungary were the German auto giants Opel and Audi. Another significant investment came from the Italian airline Alitalia, which bought a large share of MALEV, Hungary's national airline. Total foreign investment by 1994 reached $7 billion, half of the total foreign investment in Eastern Europe. Of that, business from the United States accounted for $3.6 billion, far more than businesses from any other country. Many Hungarian firms, with highly skilled employees working for low wages, were becoming competitive and exporting successfully. By 1994 about 70 percent of Hungary's trade was with the West, especially with Germany.

On the other hand, many Hungarian industries that had sold their products to the other Eastern European Communist countries or the former Soviet Union were forced to close down when those markets shrank or disappeared entirely.

The government also tried to deal with the painful legacy of Hungary's previous half century. By 1992 parliament had passed laws providing compensation for people whose property had been seized between 1939 and 1989. This included seizures by both the World War II-era fascist regime and the Cold War Communist regime. Another important piece of legislation dealing with sensitive political matters allowed for the prosecution of state officials who committed crimes during the 1956 revolution.

Despite this undeniable progress and willingness to face difficult issues, other developments weakened the Antall government's popular support. The decline of the economy through 1993 hurt many groups, including ordinary working people and the elderly. The unemployed struggled to survive, while ordinary workers worried about losing their jobs. The economic recovery that began in 1994 did not come soon enough to help the government. In addition, there was a scandal over alleged interference by government officials in the state-controlled radio and television companies and other branches of the media. The confusion of the immediate post-Communist era made some people idealize the past, including the authoritarian era between the world wars. An extreme nationalist group developed inside the Hungarian Democratic Forum (HDF) led by its vice-chairman Istvan Csurka. His program of promoting what he called "Hungarianness" included fanatic nationalism and anti-Semitism. In July 1993 the tension reached the point where Csurka quit the HDF and formed his own ultranationalist party, the Hungarian Justice and Life Party. Five months later Jozsef Antall died after a long illness. He was replaced as prime minister by Dr. Peter Boross, an independent politician who had been serving as interior minister.

The Socialists Return to Power

By 1994 the Hungarian Socialist Party (HSP) had undergone major changes. Its program and approach to the voters more closely resembled the democratic socialist parties of Western Europe than the Communist parties of the former Soviet bloc. It repeatedly assured the voters that it was not going to turn back the clock to Communism. Rather, it promised to continue reforms, but at the same time to provide more help to those hurt or threatened by economic change. More than 60 percent of the voters turned out for the election. Many who chose to remember the economic security rather than the repression of the Communist era responded to the HSP message. They gave the party 209 seats in the parliament, an absolute majority. The Hungarian Democratic Forum won only 37 seats. To further strengthen its position, the HSP formed a coalition with the Alliance of Free Democrats, the second-place finisher in the election with 70 parliamentary seats. It joined with the socialists after receiving a guarantee that the government would continue with economic reforms, especially privatization and tax incentives for foreign investors. Three other parties, all strongly antisocialist, won at least 5 percent of the vote.

The new prime minister was HSP leader Gyula Horn. He had been a well-known Communist reformer in the 1980s and, as he reminded voters, played a major role in opening Hungary's border to Austria and thereby piercing the Iron Curtain in 1989. The new government continued to push economic reform. It tried to hold down wages and, beginning in 1995, to speed privatization, as well as to cut the budget deficit. These programs were reasonably successful. The economy grew, although slowly, during 1995 and 1996. The rate of growth increased in 1997. That year privatization was almost completed. Meanwhile, total direct foreign investment reached a hefty $16 billion.

At the same time, attempts to cut the budget deficit by reducing spending on welfare and social security met with protests. In early 1995 several government ministers resigned in disagreement over spending cuts, and a large demonstration took place in Budapest. In 1996 there was a major scandal involving corruption in the privatization process. Prime Minister Horn responded firmly. He fired his privatization minister and other leading officials connected with that office. In March 1996 the Hungarian Democratic Forum split in two. Disagreements between the Hungarian Socialist Party and its coalition partners delayed important legislation, including an outline for a new constitution. Meanwhile, small parties on the extreme left and right gained in popularity.

The government received some sorely needed good news in July 1997 when Hungary was invited to join NATO, along with Poland and the Czech Republic. Hungary was the only country of the three to hold a national referendum on the issue. When it took place in November, barely half the voters showed up at the polls. It was yet another sign, confirmed by polls and surveys, that average Hungarians were primarily interested in domestic affairs. Still, more than 85 percent of those who did vote supported NATO membership, despite concerns many had that the expense of joining the alliance was more than Hungary could afford. As one young engineer put it just before he voted, "We should be spending what money we have on education and health."[3]

Power Shifts Again

These sentiments once again were felt when Hungary's second parliamentary elections of the post-Communist era were held in May 1998. As in 1994, the voters held the government responsible for the country's economic and social problems as it struggled through its transition to a free-market economy. But in 1998 it was the Hungarian Socialist Party that suffered the electoral consequences. It finished second in the balloting with 134 seats in parliament. The first-place finisher, emerging from the pack of also-rans from four years earlier, was the Federation of Young Democrats, led by a charismatic young lawyer named Viktor Orban. Orban founded the party, popularly known as Fidesz, as a dissident movement in 1988. After a respectable showing in 1994, Fidesz prepared carefully for 1998. To win the votes of average Hungarians, it focused on economic hardship, which was widespread despite Hungary's relative prosperity, as well on as rising crime and government corruption. In the election, Fidesz won about 37 percent of the vote and 148 seats in parliament. It gathered the necessary majority to set up a government by forming a coalition with the Hungarian Democratic Forum and the Independent Smallholders, a party with a strong base among farmers and other rural voters. At age thirty-five, Viktor Orban became Hungary's prime minister.

Finding Solutions for the Future

Prime Minister Orban faced a full agenda as he began his term in office. He could take pride that, in March 1999, Hungary officially joined NATO. Yet while Hungary was one of the most prosperous countries in Eastern Europe, and although the toughest days of market reform appeared to be over, life was still not easy for many Hungarians. As one small businessman put it, "The politicians better pay attention to what's happening in everyday life."[4] That "everyday life" included a growing crime wave in which criminal gangs used car bombs in their wars with each other, including one that shook one of Hungary's working-class neighborhoods during the 1998 election campaign. Hungary's disturbing new everyday life also included the gunning down of a prominent publisher in broad daylight, a series of bombings—in nightclubs, cafés, and the homes of two leading politicians—government corruption, and increasingly visible evidence of how hard economic reform was on many Hungarians who lacked the skills demanded by the modern free marketplace. The owner of a Budapest flower shop described how that hardship was affecting not only her business, but her entire world:

> It's disillusionment. Fewer and fewer people are buying flowers, and I see more and more people rummaging in that trash bin over there. You hear reports about scandals—and we're still struggling to get by.[5]

Everyday life also included increasing intolerance, at least among Hungarians frustrated by what they were experiencing and looking for easy answers to their problems. That intolerance was reflected in the success of Istvan Csurka's ultranationalist and anti-Semitic Hungarian Justice and Life Party, which in the 1998 elections reached the 5 percent threshold necessary to win a share of the proportional representation seats in parliament. Intolerance and bigotry flared into violence in early 1999, when hundreds of neo-Nazis fought with police in the center of Budapest, injuring eight officers.

Another division running through Hungarian life had to do with the secrets of the past. Although some former Communist countries were opening the records of the Communist-era secret police, Hungary lagged behind. This was especially true after the Hungarian Socialist Party, whose leaders obviously had plenty to hide, came to power in 1994. In fact, a great many Hungarians, even those not associated with the former Communist regime, had something to hide. After all, almost anyone who wanted to get along had to make compromises with the Communist dictatorship. Still, prominent Hungarians stressed the need to come to terms with the past, however unpleasant. Among them was Imre Mecs, a member of parliament who spent six years on death row after the 1956 uprising. As he put it:

> The process has only begun—we have to force it open. I
> feel that the past should be opened as a cleansing process.
> It will hurt personal feelings, but these are things we have
> to swallow.[6]

These conditions—social, economic, and moral—were taking their toll despite Hungary's unmistakable progress in its first post-Communist decade. They underlined the importance of remarks that Viktor Orban made while campaigning to lead his country in the spring of 1998:

> Our task was difficult. We had to prove that there are
> alternative leaders in Hungary and we had to persuade
> voters that there are solutions to the problems they are
> experiencing.[7]

Orban succeeded in persuading the voters. His ability to deliver on his promises would play an important role in determining how Hungary begins the new millennium.

Chapter

The Czech Republic and the Slovak Republic

The Czechs and Slovaks are descendants of Slavic tribes that migrated to their current homes near the geographic center of Europe in the fifth century. The regions of Bohemia and Moravia, where the tribes who became today's Czechs settled, now constitute the Czech Republic. Slovakia lies directly to the east. The two peoples speak closely related languages that are mutually understandable, that is, despite certain differences a Czech speaker can understand a Slovak speaker and vice versa.

During the mid-seventh century the Slavic tribes living in Slovakia and parts of Moravia were part of a kingdom ruled by a Frankish merchant and warrior named Samo. This loosely organized kingdom, the region's first Slavic state, lasted only thirty years before collapsing after Samo's death in 658. The first substantial state that united Czechs and Slovaks was the Great Moravian Empire, which existed from 833 to until 907. Although missionaries came from both Rome and Byzantium to convert the Slavs, the Great Moravian Empire accepted Roman Catholicism.

A Magyar invasion destroyed the Great Moravian Empire in 907. Thereafter, despite a religious link to Western culture, the Czechs and Slovaks were pulled in different directions for ten centuries. For about five hundred years they belonged to different kindgoms. After 1526 they both came under Hapsburg rule. Yet even then the Czechs were most directly subject to German and the Slovaks to Hungarian influence. More than a thousand years passed between the collapse of the Great Moravian Empire and the founding of Czechoslovakia in 1918, when Czechs and Slovaks finally were again united in an independent state. This long period of separation had helped create distinct Czech and Slovak identities and therefore, in turn, contributed to the breakup of Czechoslovakia after the fall of Communism.

Czech History to 1918

A Czech state in Bohemia established its independence in the ninth century, just before the destruction of the Great Moravian Empire. Eventually the new state won control of Moravia and immediately faced a challenge that became a basic theme in Czech history: the struggle for independence under constant German pressure from the west. In fact, after 950, Bohemia was part of the German-dominated, although loosely structured, Holy Roman Empire. The Bohemian Kingdom grew stronger during the thirteenth century, a period marked by large-scale German immigration, especially into the region's towns. In the fourteenth century Bohemia's founding Czech dynasty died out and was replaced by the non-Czech Luxembourg dynasty. It was under the second Luxembourg monarch, Charles IV (1342–1378), that the Bohemian Kingdom reached its peak. Charles was crowned Holy Roman emperor in 1355 and increased Bohemia's influence within the empire. He also developed Bohemia itself. Charles founded Charles University, the first university in Eastern Europe, in Prague, Bohemia's capital. He completed several major building projects in Prague, including the Cathedral of St. Vitus and a new area called the New Town, that both beautified and expanded the city. Bohemia and Moravia flourished during his reign. Therefore, although Charles himself was not a Czech and focused much of his energy on the Holy Roman Empire, his initiatives there began what is considered the "Golden Age" of Czech history.

The Bohemian Kingdom weakened under Charles's successors. Meanwhile, a powerful movement with both religious and national implications was taking shape. Its leader was Jan Huss (1372–1415), a reformist preacher and rector of Charles University. Echoing John Wycliffe of England, Huss attacked abuses and corruption in the Roman Catholic Church. Like Wycliffe, Huss preached doctrines that would play a central role in the Protestant Reformation that swept Europe in the sixteenth cen-

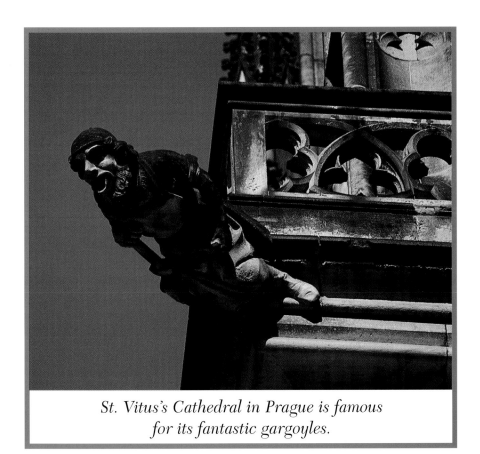

St. Vitus's Cathedral in Prague is famous for its fantastic gargoyles.

tury. The Hussite movement also had a powerful national thrust as it strongly affirmed Czech identity against German influence and pressure. A brilliant speaker, Huss broke with tradition and delivered his sermons in Czech and also translated hymns and songs into his native language. He thereby modernized spoken Czech and helped turn it into a written language. Huss angered and frightened the Papacy and was burned at the stake as a heretic at its Council of Constance in 1415. The anniversary of his death, July 6, remains a national Czech holiday.

The Hussite movement outlived its founder and survived the twenty years of religious war in Bohemia that followed his death. But the political fortunes of the Czechs were declining. The second half of the fifteenth century was a period of political instability. After the Ottoman Turks conquered Hungary, the Bohemian Kingdom fell under the rule of the Hapsburg Empire. During the rest of the century and into the next, the Czech lands were lashed by the storms of the Protestant Reformation and Catholic Counter-Reformation. The Thirty Years' War (1618–1648), the last of Europe's religious wars that devastated the Holy Roman Empire, actually began in Prague as a Czech revolt against Hapsburg rule. In 1620, Czech forces were crushed by Hapsburg troops at the decisive Battle of White Mountain. Severe repression followed. There were efforts to get Czechs to speak German and to encourage the immigration of Germans into Bohemia. There also was a largely successful attempt to re-Catholicize those Czechs who had adopted Protestantism.

Not until the late 1700s and early 1800s would the Czechs actively begin to recover their national and cultural traditions in what is called the National Revival. A key step in that effort was the founding of the Museum of the Bohemian Kingdom in 1818. The National Revival's most important figure was the historian Frantisek Palacky (1798–1876), the Czech leader during the Revolutions of 1848. The repressed state of Czech culture and the Czech language in the early nineteenth century is dramatically illustrated by the fact that the first volume of Palacky's monumental five-volume history of the Czech people were written in German. Although Palacky's efforts and the democratic revolutionaries were defeated in 1848–1849, the decades that followed saw extensive industrialization in the Czech lands. Economic development promoted the growth of a middle class, which in turn promoted Czech cultural development and national feeling.

The Czechs did not, however, benefit politically from the reforms that produced the Dual Monarchy of Austria-Hungary in 1867. They continued to be subject to Austrian political control and cultural domination. It took World War I, which shattered Austria-Hungary, to restore Czech independence.

Slovak History to 1918

In sharp contrast to the Czechs, the Slovaks were unable to establish any sort of political independence after the fall of the Great Moravian Empire. Instead, its collapse marked the beginning of almost a thousand years of Slovak political subjugation to the Hungarians. The Hungarians annexed Slovakia to their newly established Kingdom of Hungary early in the eleventh century. Under Hungarian rule, most Slovaks remained peasants while the majority of the town dwellers in Slovakia were Germans or Jews. When the Ottoman Turks overran most of Hungary after 1526, and Slovakia, along with western Hungary, fell under Hapsburg rule, Slovakia continued to be dominated by Hungarian nobles who owned most of the land. Bratislava, Slovakia's major city, where the Hungarian king Matthias Corvinus had founded a university in 1467, even served as Hungary's capital. During the following centuries the Slovaks were subject to both Germanization and Hungarianization pressures.

A genuine Slovak national revival did not get started until early in the nineteenth century. Some of the intellectuals involved in that movement had a broad outlook that stressed the unity of Czechs and Slovaks. Others chose to break with the Czechs; their efforts included developing a distinctly Slovak literary language. In any event, the Slovaks' main problems continued to be with the Hungarians. During the Revolutions of 1848 the Slovaks found out that even when Hungarians were struggling for their own freedom and for democracy, they remained hostile to Slovak national hopes. Hungarian attempts to assimilate the Slovaks increased after the establishment of the Dual Monarchy of Austria-Hungary in 1867. For example, in 1907, Hungary became the sole language of elementary education in Slovakia. Many Slovaks responded by leaving their homes and immigrating to the United States, where they continued to support Slovakian freedom from Austria-Hungary.

The efforts of those who stressed unity bore fruit in the fall of 1918 when Czech and Slovak leaders came together to establish the independent country of Czechoslovakia.

Czechoslovakia, 1918–1948

Czechoslovakia was the major political and economic success story of Eastern Europe in the two decades following World War I. It developed and maintained Eastern Europe's only stable democratic government. The central figure in that effort was Czech leader Thomas Masaryk (1850–1937). During the war he succeeded in bringing Czech and Slovak leaders together to work to create an independent state that would unite both peoples. On October 28, 1918, the founding of Czechoslovakia was announced in Prague. Two weeks later Masaryk became his country's first president. Masaryk, who enjoyed great popularity and respect, provided Czechoslovakia with the effective leadership it needed to build a new nation. Having inherited three quarters of all industry in the fallen Austro-Hungarian Empire, Czechoslovakia also boasted Eastern Europe's most industrially developed and prosperous economy.

However, Czechoslovakia had serious domestic problems it was unable to solve. It was seriously weakened because it was a multicultural country whose population of 14 million lacked a majority nationality. There were about 5.5 million Czechs, 3.5 million Slovaks, 3.1 million Germans, 750,000 Hungarians, and about 1 million people belonging to smaller minority groups. From the start, Czechoslovakia's multiculturalism tore at the country's unity. Its ethnic Germans, most of whom lived in the mountainous Sudetenland region bordering Germany and Austria, openly opposed the postwar territorial arrangements that had left them in Czechoslovakia. So did the country's ethnic Hungarians. The Slovaks believed that Czechoslovakia's centralized government denied them the autonomy they had been promised. They resented the Czechs, who were generally more prosperous than the Slovaks, accusing them of dominating the country's political life.

In the end, however, Czechoslovakia was destroyed not by internal problems but by foreign aggression and Western cowardice. In 1933 Adolf Hitler and the Nazi Party came to power in Germany. Within a few years Germany was threatening its neighbors. In 1938 Hitler demanded that Czechoslovakia cede the Sudetenland to Germany. Desperate to avoid war, Great Britain and France then disgraced themselves when they agreed to Hitler's demands at the Munich Conference of September 1938. Deserted by the Western democracies, Czechoslovakia had no choice but to comply. A few months later, in March 1938, Germany occupied Bohemia and Moravia. It then set up a puppet Slovak state under a pro-Nazi regime headed by a Catholic priest named Josef Tizo.

Of course, Britain, France, and the rest of Europe were unable to avoid war. Continued German expansion led to the outbreak of World War II in September 1939. With Nazi Germany's defeat in 1945 Czechoslovakia was restored to the map minus its easternmost tip which was annexed by the Soviet Union. The Sudeten Germans, who now were considered an unacceptable security threat, were expelled and replaced by Czech settlers. But Czechoslovakia's freedom was short-lived, a victim this time of Soviet aggression and the mounting tensions of the Cold War. In February 1948, the Communist Party of

Czechoslovakia, backed by the Soviets, overthrew the country's democratic government and established a Soviet-dominated Communist dictatorship that would control Czechoslovakia for the next forty-one years.

Czechoslovakia Under Communism

The Czechoslovak Communist regime set up in 1948 was a hard-line dictatorship. It did not introduce significant reforms until the 1960s, well after the death of Soviet dictator Joseph Stalin. Ultimately, widespread unrest produced one of the most unexpected and remarkable episodes of the Soviet era in Eastern Europe. In January 1968 the Communist Party chose Alexander Dubcek, a Slovak with a reputation as a reformer, as its new leader. Over the next several months Dubcek and his team began implementing reforms far beyond those yet seen anywhere in the Soviet bloc. Dubcek promised genuine democratic elections, freedom of expression, and a sharply reduced role for the Communist Party in the lives of the people. He called his program "socialism with a human face." However, what the people of Czechoslovakia and around the world called the "Prague Spring" the Soviet leadership saw as a threat to its control over Eastern Europe and even a danger to the Soviet Union's Communist dictatorship. The Soviets reacted with brutal efficiency in August 1968 by invading Czechoslovakia with about 600,000 Warsaw Pact troops. Dubcek was removed from office and expelled from the party, but not imprisoned or executed, as Imre Nagy had been in Hungary a decade earlier. Dubcek's replacement as party leader was fellow Slovak Gustav Husak, a colorless bureaucrat who restored a dreary Soviet-style order and dutifully followed Moscow's directions for the next two decades. Still, some Czechoslovakians would not be silenced. Among them was a group of dissidents, including a playwright named Vaclav Havel, who together in 1977 formed the human-rights group Charter 77.

The End of Communism

Beginning in 1985, the pressure for reform came from an unexpected place: the Soviet Union, where Mikhail Gorbachev was trying to revitalize his country. The conservative party leadership in Czechoslovakia held out against real change. Growing frustration led to demonstrations, and after one such demonstration in February 1989, the authorities arrested Havel and sentenced him to nine months in prison. Strong international reaction forced the regime to release him in May, and more antigovernment demonstrations followed. By early fall, the Communist regimes in Poland and Hungary had fallen, and the East German government was on the verge of collapse. On November 17, police in Prague violently broke up a demonstration by 50,000 students, the largest protest in Czechoslovakia since 1968. Five hundred people were injured that day. But the government's brutality did it no good. As Ivan Klima, a novelist whose writings the government had banned since 1968, put it:

> The regime, unable to discern its utter isolation . . . reacted
> in its usual manner to a peaceful demonstration. . . . It
> could not have picked a worse moment—the patience of
> a silent nation had snapped; the circumstances had finally
> changed.[1]

After November 17 the process of change was largely peaceful, which is why Czechoslovakians called their overthrow of Communism the "velvet revolution." Events accelerated extremely quickly. On November 19, Havel took the lead in forming a new opposition group, Civic Forum. Its headquarters, befitting a playwright and the remarkable drama he was helping to create, was the Magic Lantern Theater, located in central Prague in the basement of a stone building decorated with huge gargoyles. The next day 250,000 people demonstrated peacefully in Prague. On November 22, 1989, after twenty-one years of silence, Alexander Dubcek spoke to a enthusiastic rally in

Bratislava. He then came to Prague, where 500,000 people were staging a three-day rally against the government. On November 27, millions of people throughout the country—from Prague and Bratislava to small industrial towns—walked off their jobs at noon in a massive two-hour general strike that brought the country to a standstill. It was a crushing blow against the Communists, whose claim to power and legitimacy was based on the support of blue-collar workers. The final victory came in December. On December 10 the government was reorganized to give Czechoslovakia its first majority non-Communist government since 1948. In the last days of 1989, the parliament elected Vaclav Havel as president of Czechoslova-

A Czechoslovakian student holds a picture of Vaclav Havel in 1989 during the Velvet Revolution.

kia. The parliament then elected Alexander Dubcek as its speaker. Czechoslovakia now began a new era, free of Communism but not of other threats to its well-being and, as it turned out, to its very existence.

Czechoslovakia's Short Post-Communist History

In January 1990, President Havel gave his first New Year's Address to his countrymen. It was a remarkable speech by an extraordinary man who in the coming years would provide a rare example of how to combine political and moral leadership. Havel reminded the nation that for forty years the Communists had not told them the truth. He then set a new standard, one that he would meet, when he said, "I assume you did not propose me for this office so that I, too, would lie to you."[2]

One of first actions of the new government was symbolic, but still enormously important. In April parliament officially renamed the country the Czech and Slovak Federative Republic. The new name was designed to satisfy Slovak demands for equal status in the newly liberated nation. Although the central government in Prague still ran the country, it was divided into parts similar to U.S. states: the Czech Republic with its capital in Prague and the Slovak Republic with its capital in Bratislava. Each also had a local parliament and government, a leftover from the Communist era.

In June 1990, Czechoslovakia held its first free elections since 1946. The winners, among twenty-seven political parties and movements, were Civic Forum in the Czech Republic and its allied group, Public Against Violence (PAV), in the Slovak Republic. Between them they won a majority in the national parliament, the Federal Assembly. The election was seen as a transitional step; therefore, deputies were elected to two-year terms. Beginning in 1992 the term of office was to be four years. The new prime minister was Marian Calfa, a former Communist. The important post of finance minister, the official in charge of economic policy, was Vaclav Klaus, a strong advocate of free-market reforms. In July the parliament reelected Havel as the country's president.

During 1990 and 1991 most prices were decontrolled, thousands of small businesses were privatized, and some inefficient state enterprises were closed. The government also introduced a voucher system to privatize large state enterprises. These steps caused the usual hardships: rapid price increases that outran wages, unemployment, and falling industrial production. The standard of living fell, often sharply. The reforms were most severe in Slovakia, the poorer part of the country and home to many of the inefficient Communist-era factories hardest hit by economic change. By the end of 1991 unemployment in Slovakia was almost triple that in the Czech Republic, while the fall in industrial output was a third larger. This intensified Slovak ethnic resentment against Czechs, which in turn opened the door to politicians ready to exploit ethnic differences and tensions to increase their power. By 1991 the leading Slovak politician playing the ethnic card was Vladimir Meciar. A founder of the PAV, Meciar in 1991 broke away to form a separate political party, the Movement for a Democratic Slovakia (MDS), dedicated to expanding Slovak autonomy. At the same time, policy disagreements split Civic Forum into the Civic Democratic Party (CDP), led by Vaclav Klaus, and the Civic Movement officially led by Havel.

While all this was going on, Czechoslovakia worked on its relations with the outside world. In January 1991 it joined with Hungary and Poland in leaving the Warsaw Pact, which was officially dissolved four months later. President Havel meanwhile pushed strongly for the withdrawal of the 80,000 Soviet troops still in his country, and they were out by the end of the year, just as the Soviet Union itself was collapsing. Czechoslovakia also formed the informal group Visigrad with Poland and Hungary to work on regional problems. That effort was part of a broader goal to win membership in the European Union.

Another key goal was to join NATO, the Western alliance that had contained Soviet power during the Cold War, which Czechoslovakia and its neighbors now saw as a guarantee against future efforts by Russia to reassert its power in Eastern Europe.

By mid-1992 Czechoslovakia's ethnic tensions, exploited and expanded by Meciar and other Slovak nationalists, was becoming critical. The elections of June 1992 made matters worse by strengthening Meciar and demonstrating that there was no political party in Czechoslovakia with a power base that included both Czechs and Slovaks. Slovak politicians now demanded political changes that would have turned the federal government into an empty shell. Some Czechs, such as Vaclav Klaus, who became prime minister in July, began to think that the Czechs might be better off without the Slovaks. Havel strongly disagreed, but his position was weakened in July 1992 when parliament refused to reelect him as president. Although still president pending the election of someone else, Havel nonetheless resigned, having given up hope of preserving Czechoslovakia's unity. He was not replaced, as no other leaders stepped forth as presidential candidates.

The irony of what happened next is that polls showed that only one third of the country's people favored a breakup. Even some Slovak leaders, surprised that Klaus and his supporters were ready to see them leave, seemed less interested in a final split. But ethnic politics had been pushed too far, and politicians who favored the dissolution, such as Meciar and Klaus, used their power to block a national referendum on the issue. On November 25, 1992, the federal parliament passed a law splitting Czechoslovakia into two independent countries. Just two years had passed from the rare peaceful "velvet revolution" to the equally rare, but decidedly sadder, peaceful "velvet divorce." On December 31, Czechoslovakia officially ceased to exist. In its place were the Czech Republic and the Slovak Republic, each independent but also alone.

The Czech Republic

Although the Czech Republic that was born in 1993 was the result of the political failure that destroyed Czechoslovakia, it began its history as an independent country in better shape than most of its Eastern European neighbors who had been on their own since 1989. Despite economic recession that began in the late 1990s and lasted into the new century, ten years after Communism and seven years after the "velvet divorce," the Czech Republic stood, along with Poland and Hungary, as one of the region's post-Communist successes.

Geography and People

The Czech Republic has an area of 30,450 square miles (78,865 square kilometers), about 60 percent of the former Czechoslovakia and slightly smaller than the state of South Carolina. It includes the traditional Czech "crown lands" of Bohemia and Moravia, as well as a part of historic Silesia, the majority of which belongs to Poland. Prague is its capital and largest city. The other major cities, Ostrava and Brno, are located in the country's northeastern and southeastern corners, respectively.

The Czech Republic is divided into two main geographic areas. In the west is the Bohemian Plateau, surrounded by a series of low mountain ranges that mark large sections of the country's borders with Germany and Poland. Thus the Bohemian Forest in the southwest and the Ore Mountains in the northeast divide the Czech Republic from Germany, while the Giant Mountains in the northeast border on Poland. A band of hills called the Bohemian-Moravian Heights separates Bohemia from the Czech Republic's other main region, the fertile Moravian lowlands in the eastern part of the country. Mountains near the Polish border in turn separate Moravia from the Czech Republic's small corner of Silesia. In the east, the Carpathian Mountains separate Moravia and the Czech Republic from Slovakia.

*The Vlatava River passes through the center of Prague,
giving the city some of its most picturesque views.*

The Czech Republic has three main rivers. The Vlatava passes through Prague on its northward course to meet the Labe, the Czech portion of the Elbe River that eventually crosses Germany en route to the North Sea. The Morava River flows southward out of the Czech Republic, becoming the Czech border with Slovakia, and then the Slovak border with Austria, before flowing into the Danube. What all these rivers, and most of the Czech Republic's other rivers, have in common is that they are badly polluted by sewage and agricultural runoff.

The Czech Republic has a continental climate with warm summers and cold, often cloudy, winters. Dense fogs, which are frequently turned into thick smog by pollution, are common during the winter months. The country is self-sufficient in food.

Its main products are livestock, grains, vegetables, poultry, potatoes, and sugar beets. The main agricultural regions are the Moravian lowlands and the river valleys of the Vlatava and Labe. One of the Czech Republic's main natural resources is soft brown coal, which is taken from huge open-pit mines in the northern part of the country. That coal, used in industries and homes, is one of the main sources of the country's terrible pollution problem. Other natural resources include hard coal, clay, and bauxite, the ore from which aluminum is produced. Czech industries produce iron, steel, machinery and equipment, motor vehicles, glass, and armaments. A recent success has been the revival of the famous Bata shoe factory, founded in 1894, which today produces more than 250,000 pairs of shoes per week.

The Czech Republic is an overwhelmingly homogeneous country. Ethnic Czechs make up more than 94 percent of the

For a 1990 visit from Pope John Paul II, Slovakians in traditional dress line the parade route.

population of 10.3 million people. Three percent of the population are Slovaks. There are very small communities of Germans, Poles, Gypsies, Hungarians, and a few other minority groups. In terms of religious affiliation, almost 40 percent of the population identify themselves as atheist. Almost as many are Catholics, while 4.6 percent are Protestant and 3 percent are Orthodox.

History Since 1993

The Czech Republic began its life with a new constitution adopted in December 1992. The new constitution provided for a bicameral legislature with a 200-member Chamber of Deputies as the lower house and an 81-member Senate as the upper house. The Chamber of Deputies is elected according to proportional representation, while the Senate's members are elected from single-member districts. Executive power is held by a council of ministers headed by the prime minister, a post initially filled by former Czechsolvakian prime minister Vaclav Klaus. However, the president, elected for a five-year term, also holds considerable authority. In January 1993 the Chamber of Deputies, whose members, like the prime minister, were holdovers from the Czechoslovakian era, elected Vaclav Havel as the Czech Republic's first president. The government's priorities remained largely the same as before, including continuing privatization and other economic reforms, fighting the growing menace of organized crime, and dealing with the country's environmental problems. A new objective was to normalize relations with Slovakia.

The Czech's Republic's economy grew slowly in 1993 and 1994, then by an excellent 5.9 and 4.1 percent during 1995 and 1996. Inflation and unemployment did not become major problems. This was due in part to Klaus's policy of decreasing state control gradually in order to avoid economic hardship. President Havel sometimes differed with Prime Minister Klaus's policies, with the president favoring more emphasis on social welfare and the prime minister pushing a faster pace toward a complete free-market economy. In any event, by 1995 about 80 percent of the economy was in private hands, an impressive achievement. Still, it turned out that there were two serious and closely related drawbacks to the Klaus program. First, despite privatization, the state still maintained a controlling interest in many large industrial businesses and banks. Second, many of those enterprises were unreformed; that is, they were run by the same bureaucrats who ran them before 1989 or they were controlled by investment funds known for shady stock deals.

The first-ever parliamentary elections in the history of the Czech Republic took place in 1996. Klaus's Civic Democratics finished first with 29.5 percent of the vote, good for 68 Chamber of Deputies seats. In reality, however, that was a setback, since the party and its coalition partners won only 99 of chamber's 200 seats. This left the Klaus government in jeopardy. The main opposition party, the Czech Social Democratic Party (CSDP), placed second by winning 26 percent of the vote and quadrupling its strength in parliament to 61 seats. It had begun its existence as a refuge for former Communists, but by 1996 had attracted new members and evolved into a traditional Western European social democratic party. The Social Democrats favored a slowdown in market reforms. Only timely intervention by President Havel helped forge an agreement under which the Social Democrats would support the coalition on key issues and thereby allow it to continue to govern. The coalition did better in the November Senate elections, winning a majority of the seats.

The next month the president was once again in the news, but for a very frightening reason. On December 2, Vaclav Havel, a long-time heavy smoker, underwent surgery for lung cancer. The four-hour operation was a success, but Havel's health now became a national concern. It remained a front-page issue throughout 1997, when he suffered from bouts of pneumonia and bronchitis, and in 1998, when he underwent emergency intestinal surgery.

The year 1997 was not an easy one for the Czech Republic. A rare bright spot was the republic's invitation to join NATO in July, which Havel had worked so hard to get. On the negative side, economic growth dropped to less than 2 percent, in part because of severe floods in July. Both unemployment and inflation increased, while foreign investment fell. The country also was rocked by political scandal, including corruption linked to the privatization process and campaign financing. In December, President Havel complained that power was "again in the hands of untrustworthy figures whose primary concern is their personal advancement instead of the interest of the people."[3] But Havel did not criticize only politicians and big bankers. He warned the country as a whole that it was failing in what he called "human relations," that is, the way people treat each other. He was especially concerned about violence against the country's Gypsy community, by "the dreadful behavior of some of our people toward their fellow humans simply because of the different color of their skin."[4] In any event, the campaign finance scandal forced Klaus to resign as prime minister. Havel named Josef Tosovsky, a respected banker who did not belong to any political party, as interim prime minister. Meanwhile, new elections were scheduled for June of 1998.

The year 1998 began with Havel's reelection as president. However, it was a sign of the growing division in the country that it took him two ballots in both houses of parliament to get the votes he needed. The June parliamentary elections also revealed a divided country. The Social Democrats, led by Milos Zeman, campaigned on themes that included slowing down privatization, increasing the minimum wage, and expanding welfare services. They won a narrow plurality, just a few percentage points more than the Civic Democrats. After several weeks of maneuvering, Zeman was named prime minister and formed a new government. However, that government depended on the support of former prime minister Klaus and the Civic Democrats. How Zeman, a critic of many free-market reforms, would work with Klaus, the free-market advocate, was an open question.

By the year 2000, it was fair to say that the Czech Republic, which officially joined NATO in March 1999, had established its place among Europe's democratic community of nations. However, this achievement did not diminish the country's serious economic problems and growing political divisions. These troubles cost President Havel some of his luster. His approval rating, which for years stood at 80 percent, by late 1999 had fallen to barely 50 percent. To many Czechs, the former dissident leader was now part of the political establishment. Havel himself was philosophical about it all. He observed that ten years earlier he had become president "as a service for my country." While Havel admitted that "the service is much harder than I expected when I accepted it," and while he certainly regretted certain mistakes, Havel had no regrets about his decision to accept the burden of leadership:

> The question whether I regret is like asking me whether I regret that I was born. It's simply a part of my life. I take it as a fact.[5]

The Slovak Republic

The Slovak Republic is the smaller and poorer part of the former Czechoslovakia. It also is the part where democratic traditions are weaker. The political problems that have developed as a result have been a major cause of the difficulties that Slovaks have faced in their first decade of post-Communism and independence.

Geography and People

The Slovak Republic has an area of 18,933 square miles (49,035 square kilometers), about twice the size of New Hampshire. The northwestern section of the Carpathian Mountains runs through central and northern parts of the country. The highest peak in this rugged and forested area, standing 8,710 feet (2,655 meters) above sea level, is called Gerlachovka. It is in a range called the High Tatra near Slovakia's border with Poland. About 80 percent of the country is more than 2,400 feet (750 meters) above sea level. South of the mountains and hills toward the Hungarian border are fertile lowlands. They are drained by the Danube and some of its tributaries, the most important of which is the Vah. Slovakia's rich farmland enables farmers to grow wheat and other grains, potatoes, sugar beets, hops, and fruits, and to raise cattle, poultry, and hogs. Slovakia has warm summers and cold cloudy winters, which are especially severe in the mountain regions.

Despite serious deforestation, about 40 percent of Slovakia still is covered by forests. They are home to a variety of wildlife, including bears, wolves, otters, mink, deer, and eagles. Slovakia's mountain pastures have long been used for sheep grazing. The forests and mountains also cover valuable mineral resources, such as high-grade iron, manganese, lead, zinc, and copper. There also are deposits of poor-quality brown coal. These resources have been the basis of Slovakia's industrial development, most of which took place under the Communist regime. The leading industries included mining, steel and steel products, machinery, chemicals, engineering, and the manufacture of nuclear fuel. Consumer industries included textiles and footwear. The Communists also built huge arms and munitions factories in Slovakia because it was near the Soviet border. These factories have suffered since 1989 because they lost their traditional Soviet bloc markets. It also has proved difficult to convert them to civilian production. Another downside of the Communist-era factories, which were built without regard for anything except the regime's immediate needs, is the serious environmental damage they have caused. Hydroelectric dams provide a significant part of Slovakia' electricity, as does a Soviet-designed nuclear power station

Slovakia has a population of slightly more than 5.4 million people, about 85 percent of whom are ethnic Slovaks. About 570,000 Hungarians form the country's largest ethnic minority. Their demands for autonomy are a major source of tension within the country and in Slovakia's relations with Hungary. Gypsies (1.5 percent) and Czechs (1 percent) are the next largest minority groups. There are smaller numbers of Ruthenians, Ukrainians, Germans, Russians, and several other groups. About 60 percent of Slovakia's people are Roman Catholics, 8.4 percent Protestants, and 4.1 percent Orthodox. About one in ten Slovakians identify themselves as atheist.

Slovakia was mainly a rural nation until the Communist era, when large-scale urbanization accompanied industrialization. Bratislava (population 450,000) is Slovakia's capital and largest city. Located just inside Slovakia's border with Austria, it is one of the country's two major industrial centers. The other is the steel-making city of Kosice, Slovakia's second-largest urban area (population 240,000) in the eastern part of the country close to the Hungarian border.

The Slovak Republic's History Since 1993

The Slovak Republic began its life without Alexander Dubcek, its most respected political figure, who died in a car accident in November 1992. Its leadership came from elections in mid-1992, which had made Vladimir Meciar's Movement for a Democratic Slovakia (MDS) the dominant party in the Slovak local parliament and led to Meciar himself becoming the republic's prime minister. It took two months of maneuvering for the parliament to elect a new president. In February 1993 it finally chose Michal Kovac, a former reformist Communist and MDS leader, who soon was feuding with the increasingly dictatorial Meciar.

Slovakia's new constitution, adopted four months before the official split with the Czechs, was a controversial document that muddied Slovakia's political waters. Written by officials schooled during the Communist era, the constitution guaranteed a list of human rights from freedom of thought, expression, and religion to the right to fair working conditions. At the same time, it also allowed those rights to be limited by laws adopted by the 150-member parliament, the National Council. Slovakia's Hungarian community protested the fact that the constitution did not protect minority rights. It was not lost on the ethnic Hungarians that the Slovak leadership, so concerned with minority rights when the Slovaks were a minority in Czechoslovakia, had no interest in the problem once they became the majority in the Slovak Republic.

It took only a few months for political feuds to break out within the MDS. A series of defections from the party forced Meciar, in order to stay in power, to form a coalition with the extreme nationalist Slovak National Party (SNP). By December he and Kovac were so at odds that Meciar called for the president's resignation. Instead, additional defections brought Meciar's government down in March 1994. By then polls showed that a majority of Slovaks regretted their split with the Czechs.

Kovac appointed former minister of foreign affairs Josef Moravcik, who a month earlier had resigned from Meciar's government and formed a new political party, as prime minister. Moravcik worked hard to encourage free-market economic reform and improve strained relations with Hungary. However, Meciar staged a comeback in the fall elections. He and the MDS proved to be skilled campaigners. They gave out free videos and cassettes, held rallies where they distributed free posters and gifts and conducted games for children, and ran sophisticated television ads designed to humanize Meciar, including one that showed him talking lovingly to his mother in her garden. Although the MDS did not win a parliamentary majority, by December Meciar had formed the coalition with the Slovak National Party and a small hard-line, prosocialist group and was back in power.

Meciar's new government immediately reversed Moravcik's pro-privatization program and soon was involved in a bitter feud with Kovac. In August 1995 it culminated in a bizarre episode in which one of Kovac's sons was kidnapped. He was taken to Austria, where he was accused of being involved in an embezzlement scheme in Germany before being released and allowed to return home. The kidnappers almost certainly were Slovakian intelligence agents working for Meciar.

The feuding grew more intense in 1995 and 1996. By then Meciar's government was being accused of a long list of human rights violations, from silencing artists and other cultural figures to trying to end freedom of the press. One organization of journalists listed him tenth on its list of the world's ten "worst enemies of the press," a list that included such figures as Cuban dictator Fidel Castro, Chinese leader Deng Xiaoping, the king of Saudi Arabia, and assorted other tyrants. In early 1998, Kovac publicly blamed the Meciar government for the country's isolation from the European mainstream and its failure to be admitted to NATO.

In March 1998, Kovac's term as president ended and he stepped down. The problem was that he was not replaced. The Slovak parliament was so divided that it could not agree on a successor. Kovac, in his farewell address, called for compromise, but to no avail. After several failed attempts, parliament gave up and opted to wait for new elections to change its composition and possibly break the deadlock.

Through it all, the Slovak economy did surprisingly well. Slovakia inherited the former Czechoslovakia's reform and privatization program that continued to move the country toward a free market after independence. Slovakia's first year on its own was difficult, as the economy continued a decline that had started back in 1990. However, by 1994 the economy started to grow and it grew strongly through 1997. By then, despite Meciar's slowing of privatization, private businesses employing 70 percent of Slovakia's workers were producing 80 percent of the country's goods and services. Much of the credit for that belonged not to the government but to ordinary Slovaks who started and developed a great variety of small businesses. On the negative side was a privatization scandal in which Meciar was accused of selling off enterprises to his cronies at bargain basement prices, about one seventh of their actual value. His government also was committed to maintaining more than 70 important enterprises—in such areas as arms production, energy, and communications—under full or partial state control.

The elections that finally brought some significant change to Slovakia's political life took place in September 1998 and May 1999. In September 1998, as 84 percent of the voters cast ballots, Meciar's MDS slipped badly and finished in a virtual dead heat with a loose alliance of democratic parties called the Slovak Democratic Union (SDK). Its leader, Mikulas Dzurinda, then cobbled together a coalition that included parties of widely differing beliefs to form a parliamentary majority and became Slovakia's new prime minister. The glue holding the flimsy coalition together was the desire to end Meciar's authoritarian rule, and Dzurinda appeared committed to following democratic rules, combating corruption, and improving Slovakia's relations with its neighbors and the countries of Western Europe. In May, Meciar suffered a second and more decisive defeat when he lost Slovakia's presidential election to Rudolf Schuster. The new president was a respected engineer and mayor of the city of Kosice. He was also the leader of the Party of Civic Understanding, one of the members of the governing coalition.

Overall, as the new century began Slovakia's record was mixed. It had made some economic progress during the 1990s, but 1999 was a poor year. There was no economic growth, and inflation and unemployment both rose. Political life had been stagnant since the breakup of Czechoslovakia, but 1998 and 1999 had produced a potential political breakthrough to democracy. There was hope for the future, but also the certainty that a lot of hard work lay ahead.

Chapter Five

Romania, Bulgaria, and Albania

Romania

Romania, the "land of the Romans," has not always ended up in the category where it properly belongs. It should be one of the richest countries in Eastern Europe. Romania has a well-educated population of 23 million people, fertile farm-land, and large oil and gas reserves. Yet it is a poor and troubled country that has been very slow to emerge from the legacy of Communism. Furthermore, Romania's designation as a Balkan country is inconsistent with the geographic facts. Inasmuch as the Danube River forms a large part of the Balkan Peninsula's northern boundary, in a technical geographical sense most of Romania lies outside the region. However, the fortunes of history have linked Romania to its neighbors to the south and southwest, so that geographers as well as historians traditionally have labeled it one of the "Balkan States."

Geography and People

Romania looks like a giant misshapen sphere about 325 miles (535 kilometers) in diameter, flattened at the top with two projections, a small pointed one in the west that pokes into Hungary and Serbia, and a large one in the southeast that connects Romania to the Black Sea. It has an area of 91,699 square miles (237,500 square kilometers), slightly smaller than Oregon.

Romania is about one-third mountain, one-third hilly country, and one-third fertile river plain, mainly the broad Danube Plain in the southern part of the country. Most of central and northern Romania is dominated by a semicircular mountain range that extends from Romania's northeast border with Ukraine across the country to its southwest border with Serbia. The northern part of the semicircle is part of the Carpathian Mountain chain. The southern, slightly higher range is the Transylvanian Alps (or Southern Carpathians). The Bihor Massif is a lower range in western Romania. Many of Romania's mountain slopes are still forested; forests still cover about 25 percent of the country. The forests, which are among the least spoiled in Europe, are home to a wide variety of wildlife including fox, deer, wild boar, and more than a hundred species of birds. About a third of Europe's lynx population (about 1,500 animals) call Romania's mountain forests home. So do 40 percent of Europe's wolves (2,500 animals) and 60 percent of the continent's brown bears (5,500 animals).

Romania comprises four main historic-geographic regions. Walachia occupies most of the country's south, minus its Black Sea coast. It is home to Bucharest, Romania's capital and largest city and the country's prized Ploiesti oil fields. Moldavia covers the northeastern part of the country, again excluding the Black Sea coast. Transylvania, an area long disputed with Hungary, makes up much of the western part of the country. A subregion in the extreme west called the Banat, which has some of

Europe's best farmland, often is included as part of Transylvania. Finally, farthest east, Romania's piece of the Black Sea coast is the northern part of a region called Dobruja, the southern part of which belongs to Bulgaria.

Romania's major river is the Danube, which drains the entire country and defines large sections of the border with Serbia and Bulgaria. The Danube flows through Romania for some 900 miles (1,450 kilometers), more than half its length. Just before reaching the Black Sea, the Danube abandons its eastward course and turns due north. It then turns east again, marking part of the Romanian-Ukrainian border before creating its huge delta as it meets the Black Sea. The Danube delta covers an area of 1,675 square miles (4,340 square kilometers) and is growing; the silt picked up in the river's long journey through Europe and deposited in its delta makes Romania about 130 feet (40 meters) longer each year. The delta has an especially diverse bird population that includes large numbers of eagles, vultures, and hawks. It is the winter home to half of the world's red-breasted geese. Most of Romania's other large rivers, including the Prut, which forms Romania's border with Moldova and Ukraine, are Danube tributaries.

Romania has cold snowy and foggy winters and warm sunny summers interrupted by frequent rainfall and thunderstorms. Natural resources, aside from oil and gas, include coal, iron ore, salt, bauxite, uranium, and timber. Among Romania's agricultural products are wheat, corn, sugar beets, sunflower seeds, grapes, meat, eggs, and milk. Its industries produce petroleum, pig iron, steel and steel products, chemical fertilizers, textiles and footwear, construction materials, electric machines, transport vehicles, and processed foods.

Romania's population is fairly homogeneous, with the exception of a large Hungarian minority. About 89 percent of the country's 22.8 million people are ethnic Romanians. The country's 1.6 million Hungarians, about 9 percent of its population, constitute the single largest minority group in Europe.

There are also more than 400,000 Gypsies in Romania, as well as smaller numbers of Germans, Ukrainians, Serbs, Croats, Russians, and Turks.

History to 1945

Romania's defining historical experience occurred in A.D. 106 when the Romans conquered the province they called Dacia. Even though the Romans withdrew under barbarian pressure in 271, their influence lasted. The native population of the region, despite being exposed to seven centuries of invasions by Goths, Huns, Slavs, Avars, Bulgars, and Magyars, continued to speak a Latin-based language that has come down to us as Romanian. Modern Romanian, notwithstanding many Slavic words, is closely related to French, Italian, and Spanish. By the eleventh century the Vlach people, ancestors of today's Romanians, who probably took refuge from invaders in the region's mountains, had resettled on Romania's plains. In the process they assimilated whatever invaders remained in the region. To this day, the Romanians take great pride in their Roman heritage and long historic ties to Western culture.

By the thirteenth century, the Hungarians controlled Transylvania, although a majority of the population remained Romanian. That century also brought devastating Mongol invasions to Romania, as it did to the rest of Eastern Europe. The fourteenth century saw the establishment of two semi-independent Romanian principalities, Walachia and Moldavia. However, in the fifteenth century, despite strong resistance, both territories became tributaries of the expanding Ottoman Empire. Even though Ottoman rule was indirect—local princes ruled as agents of the Turkish sultan—the Ottomans demanded a heavy tribute that reduced most of the population to poverty and peasant serfdom.

Romanian independence finally came in several stages in the nineteenth century. As the Ottoman Empire weakened, the powerful Russian Empire tried to increase its influence in the Balkans. The aftermath of the Crimean War (1853–1856), which involved both empires, led in 1859 to the establishment of the autonomous United Principalities of Walachia and Moldavia. Full independence came in 1878, under terms of the Treaty of Berlin. However, Romanians were angry that Russia got the Romanian-populated region of Bessarabia.

After officially becoming the Kingdom of Romania in 1881, the country made significant economic progress in the decades prior to World War I. Romania fought on the Allied side during the war, and received Transylvania, Bessarabia, and the smaller territory of Bukovina as a result. These additions doubled the country's size and population and finally united virtually all Romanians in their own state. At the same time, they gave Romania large minority populations of Hungarians, Germans, and Jews.

The interwar years in Romania were plagued by political turmoil and instability, mistreatment of minorities, and, after 1938, a dictatorship under King Carol II. When World War II began, Romania at first remained neutral. However, by 1940 a fascist, pro-German, and fiercely anti-Semitic regime led by General Ion Antonescu was in power. In 1941, Romania entered World War II on Germany's side, in part to recover Bessarabia, seized by the Soviet Union in 1940. One result was the murder of more than half of Romania's 750,000 Jews in the Holocaust. Another result, after hundreds of thousands of Romanian soldiers died fighting against the Soviet Union, was Soviet occupation of the country after Germany's defeat in 1945.

Romania Under Communism

Romania was under Soviet domination as early as 1945. However, a full-blown Communist regime did not take complete control of the country until late 1947, when King Michael was forced to abdicate and Romania was proclaimed a people's republic. After the usual Stalinist terror, collectivization, nationalization of industry and businesses, and purges, Gheorghe

Gheorghiu-Dej emerged as the country's unchallenged dictator. Gheorghiu-Dej took advantage of the withdrawal of Soviet troops in 1958 to chart a semi-independent course for Romania, while still remaining within the Soviet bloc. Instead of following Soviet wishes and making Romania a supplier of agricultural goods for other bloc members, Gheorghiu-Dej promoted industrialization. He also showed independence in foreign affairs. After his death in 1965, his successor, Nicolae Ceauşescu, continued and expanded these policies. Among Ceauşescu's independent stands was his refusal to break diplomatic relations with Israel in 1967 and to participate in the Warsaw Pact invasion of Czechoslovakia in 1968.

Ceauşescu remained in power until Communism itself fell in Romania in 1989, and the effects of his rule became increasingly damaging as time went on. He ran up Romania's foreign debt by borrowing from the West to finance extravagant industrialization and building schemes. Corruption reached a grand scale as Ceauşescu's family members—especially his wife, Elena—were given important party and state positions. By the 1980s, Romanians were suffering from serious shortages of virtually everything, from food, heat, and electricity to medicine and consumer goods. To pay its foreign debt, Romania exported food as its people went hungry and suffered in apartments without heat or electricity. As part of the Ceauşescu's campaign to increase the population, the government banned abortion and harassed women in order to get them to bear children. It persecuted Romania's Hungarian community to promote assimilation. Ceauşescu also began an agricultural development program in the Danube delta that caused enormous environmental destruction. He then destroyed a large part of historic Bucharest to build huge new government buildings, including his supposed showcase, a monstrous structure he called the House of the People.

Open protests against Ceauşescu's tyranny began as early as 1987. The Securitate, his ruthless secret police, kept matters under control. Romania's Communist regime even man-

A group of civilians surround a member of Ceauşescu's hated Securitate forces in Bucharest, 1989.

aged to buck the 1989 revolutionary trend until mid-December. The revolution finally erupted when protests began in the Transylvanian town of Timisoara. The protests continued for several days, and several hundred people reportedly were killed when security forces fired on a crowd. The protests then spread to other cities, including Bucharest. On December 21, Ceauşescu addressed a government-staged rally in the capital. As he spoke the unthinkable happened: The crowd began to boo. The formerly unchallenged dictator stood in stunned silence, his frozen image captured in a classic photo beamed around the world. The protests and fighting quickly intensified. Army units joined the protesters, and the regime finally cracked. Ceauşescu and his wife fled Bucharest in a helicopter but were captured, immediately tried by a secret military court, and executed on December 25. Fighting continued for several days. In the end Ceaușescu's defiance of his people's wishes caused the overthrow of Communism in Romania to involve more violence and take more lives than anywhere else in Eastern Europe.

Post-Communist Romania Under the National Salvation Front

One reason the Ceaușescus may have been eliminated so quickly was that other Communist leaders wanted to protect themselves. With Ceaușescu gone, they could avoid uncomfortable questions and thereby find a future in post-Communist Romania. In any event, after Ceaușescu's execution, a group called the National Salvation Front (NSF), many of whose members were former Communist officials, announced it was forming a new government. The NSF's chairman, Ion Iliescu, became Romania's new president. Iliescu had been a Ceaușescu lieutenant until he displeased his boss in 1971 by advocating reforms. The new prime minister was an academic and former Communist named Petre Roman. The NSF government introduced sweeping reforms. It immediately cancelled Ceaușescu's agricultural project in the Danube delta. It ended censorship, abolished the Communist Party, permitted non-Communist political parties, and guaranteed freedom of speech and similar rights. Trying to emphasize a break with the past, it even jailed some former Ceaușescu officials and officially disbanded the Securitate.

That break turned out to be more appearance than reality. At first the NSF had announced that it would serve only as a caretaker government and pledged not to run candidates in the parliamentary elections scheduled for May 1990. But the former Communists who ran the NSF were accustomed to holding power, and their habits did not change. In January the NSF announced it would indeed run in the elections. It also reversed its abolition of the Communist Party. When demonstrations broke out in February in Bucharest, the government brought in 3,000 miners from the northern part of the country, who supported the government because of recent pay hikes, to forcefully disperse the demonstrators. The elections then took place amid widespread harassment and intimidation. The government also exploited its control of the country's television network and the people's fear of the hardships that free-market reforms might bring. Iliescu's inflammatory language often reminded people of fascist and Communist political tactics. For example, he told miners and farmers:

> You are at the bottom of society—smash these people in the city who think they are better than you—educated, privileged.[1]

The results were predictable; the NSF won about two thirds of the seats in both houses of the bicameral parliament, and Iliescu won the presidency with 85 percent of the votes. When protest demonstrations broke out in Bucharest in June, the government again brought in the miners, this time about 7,000 of them, to beat up and scatter the demonstrators. Their attacks on the protesters left several people dead and hundreds injured. Meanwhile, the government began a few modest economic reforms, including removing price controls on many products. However, limited reforms did nothing to repair the disastrous economic conditions the Ceaușescu regime had left behind. The jump in prices following decontrol hurt ordinary working people, including the miners, who now turned against the government. Privatization, opposed by Communist-era bureaucrats who still held their jobs, barely advanced. The main change was in agriculture, where almost half the land was in private hands by 1994 and 80 percent by 1995.

The discontent showed itself in parliamentary and presidential elections held in the fall of 1992. Iliescu's Democratic National Salvation Front (the NSF had split into two factions) won about a third of the seats in parliament. A new party of genuine reformers, the Democratic Convention, finished a strong second. Iliescu was reelected president, but not without strong opposition. The Democratic Convention's candidate, Emil Constantinescu, took almost 40 percent of the vote. Overall, the elections left Iliescu and his party weaker than before.

The next four years saw continued political turmoil, social protests, and economic hardship. Romania was criticized for its treatment of its Hungarian and Gypsy minorities. It was embarrassed by a revival of anti-Semitism, especially when the government honored the memory of World War II leader Ion Antonescu, whose regime actively helped the Nazis murder Romanian Jews. Meanwhile, the government did not promote serious economic reform, and Romania's standard of living continued to fall. Less than half the economy was in private hands. Bucharest was a decaying city, its streets pocked by bathtub-size potholes. By the time the elections of 1996 were held, Romanians were tired of a government run by people who were little more than warmed-over Communists.

Constantinescu and the DCR Come to Power

In November 1996, a young university student waiting outside a polling booth explained her vote to an American reporter:

> I voted for a change. I want something new that would give people a chance to hope and to make Romania a different place for my child.[2]

It turned out the student was speaking for millions of Romanians. They made the Democratic Convention the largest party in the parliament and elected Emil Constantinescu, an internationally known geologist and a firm anti-Communist, as their country's president. As he stood on a balcony overlooking Bucharest's University Square, where protesters had been killed by both the Ceauşescu and Iliescu regimes, Constantinescu paid homage to those who had died and told his people, "Romania comes back to the great concert of democratic Europe."[3]

The day after his election Constantinescu told his people and the world:

> A hard winter is knocking at the door. We will form a government very rapidly, because the country is in a tough situation.[4]

A new coalition government was formed in December with Victor Ciorbea, who had been elected mayor of Bucharest in May 1996, as prime minister. In January, Constantinescu formed a commission to battle corruption and organized crime. The next month the government introduced a program of economic reform. But Constantinescu's prediction of a hard winter turned out to apply to the entire year of 1997 and the beginning of 1998 as well. It proved difficult to get the different parties in the government coalition to back a single economic reform plan. Despite President Constantinescu's trips abroad and meetings with political and business leaders, Romania attracted little Western investment. During 1997 the economy shrank by 6 percent; in 1998 it shrank by more than 7 percent.

Romania was also divided by a bitter debate over whether to open to the public the files of the Securitate, a step Iliescu had blocked while in power. Yet another serious unsolved problem was the status of the 1.6 million ethnic Hungarians of Transylvania. Persecuted under the Communists and considered subversives by the Iliescu regime, the Hungarians hoped for better under Constantinescu. A Hungarian-based political party even became part of the governing coalition. And, in fact, during 1997 the government issued decrees promoting bilingualism in public places and schools where Hungarians made up a fifth or more of the population. But there was strong opposition to these measures in parliament and especially among the Transylvanian Romanian community. As for the local Hungarians, they wanted even more: Their demands included a Hungarian-only university. Sadly, the only point on which Hungarians and Romanians of Transylvania agreed was their mutual dislike of another group, the local Gypsies.

The year 1999 brought Romania more hardship. In January striking coal miners staged a five-day march that led to violence in which more than 130 people were injured. It was the government's worst crisis since President Constantinescu's election. That incident was followed by two environmental disasters. In late January an estimated 100 tons of cyanide spilled from a gold smelter into a creek; the deadly poison reached four rivers, including the Danube. In March, 20,000 tons of lead and other heavy metals reached the Tizsa River when an earthen wall at a mine collapsed during heavy rains. That same month came the announcement that unemployment was at its highest level since 1990. Romania's economy was further damaged by the Kosovo crisis, which led to NATO's 78-day bombing campaign against Serbia between March and June. Lost trade and higher transport expenses cost Romania about $50 million a week. By December, ten years after the overthrow of Ceauşescu, one third of Romania's people were living on less than $2 a day.

Overall, by the year 2000, Romania had left Communism behind. It had a president committed to change. But it faced a long and very hard struggle to rebuild its national life.

Bulgaria

Bulgaria is a land of contrasts and transitions. Its geography contrasts natural features found in southern Europe with those typical of the western regions of the former Soviet Union. It is located in a part of Europe where the climate changes. Bulgaria's southern and western sections have a Mediterranean climate, while the northern and eastern regions have a colder continental climate similar to the countries of north-central Europe. It is also a country of cultural contrasts and transitions. While Bulgaria's primary cultural heritage is Slavic and Christian, a large Turkish Muslim minority lives in the eastern part of the country. Across the southeastern border is Turkey itself, and not far from the Turkish border is the Sea of Marmara, beyond which Asia begins.

Geography and People

Bulgaria is a rough rectangle about 42,855 square miles (110,994 square kilometers) in area, about the size of Tennessee, on the eastern part of the Balkan Peninsula.

Despite its relatively small size, Bulgaria has four main geographic zones. In the north is the Danubian Plain (or Bulgarian Plain), a fertile region that produces a variety of grains, vegetables, and fruits. Just to the south, spanning the country from Serbia to the Black Sea, are the Balkan Mountains, a low but rugged range that is a barrier between north and south because it is cut by only a few passes. The mountains block the cold air that pours out of northern Europe each winter, helping to give southern Bulgaria its Mediterranean climate of mild, wet winters and warm, dry summers. Heavy snowfalls cover these mountains in winter. Tucked amid these mountains is the Valley of the Roses, which supplies 70 percent of the world's rose oil used in perfumes and cosmetics. The region's other natural resources include timber, iron, and coal.

Farther south are plains, one small and one large. In the far west, overlooked by the massive snow-capped peak called Mount Vitosha, is the Sofia basin, which surrounds the city of Sofia, Bulgaria's capital and largest urban center (population about 1.1 million). Far larger and stretching across most of the country is the Thracian Plain (also called the Rumelian Lowlands). It is shaped roughly like a triangle, narrow in the west and broader in the east where it approaches the Black Sea. The Greek poet Homer called the plain the "land of fertility," and its wines were famous throughout the ancient world. Most of this bountiful agricultural region is drained by the Maritsa River, which eventually turns south and leaves Bulgaria on its journey to the Aegean Sea. The Thracian Plain produces wheat, corn, onion, tomatoes, beans, peppers, grapes, cotton, and other crops and often is called Europe's largest garden. Plovdiv, Bulgaria's second-largest city (population 379,000), stands on the banks of the Maritsa River. It has been an urban center since it was conquered by Philip II of Macedonia, father of Alexander the Great, in 341 B.C. Burgas, the country's fourth-largest city (population about 205,000) and second most important port, stands at the eastern edge of the plain overlooking a bay of the Black Sea.

Bulgaria's fourth region, in the far south along the Greek border, consists of the Rhodope Mountains, the highest and most rugged in the country. Their forested slopes are an important source of timber, while minerals such as lead, zinc, and copper lie beneath its soil. These southern mountains are capped by Mount Musala, which at 9,594 feet (2,925 meters) above sea level is the highest peak in the Balkans.

Aside from Sofia, Plovdiv, and Burgas, Bulgaria's most important city is Varna (population 315,000), on the northern part of Bulgaria's Black Sea coast. Varna, Bulgaria's main port, dates from the sixth century B.C. Today it is considered Bulgaria's summer capital. Bulgaria's Black Sea coast, with Europe's best beaches, is a major tourist attraction.

Bulgaria has another resource that has long attracted visitors: five hundred mineral springs, half of which are hot. The country's industries, mainly built during the Communist era, produce machinery, metals, petrochemicals, textiles, and some consumer goods. About 40 percent of Bulgaria's electricity comes from the Kozloduj nuclear power plant, a Soviet-era dinosaur north of Sofia that is considered one of the most dangerous in the world.

Ethnic Bulgarians make up about 85 percent of the country's population of about 8.9 million. Turks, the largest minority group, account for about 9 percent of the population. The Turks are in a difficult position. They are both a remnant and a reminder of Bulgaria's bitter experience of five hundred years under the rule of the Ottoman Empire, and there is continual tension between them and the majority Bulgarians. Another legacy of that era are the Pomaks, 250,000 descendants of Slavs who converted to Islam under the Ottomans. Gypsies and Macedonians each account for about 2.5 percent of the population. There are smaller numbers of Armenians, Russians, and other groups.

Bulgarian History to 1945

The Slavic tribes who are the main ancestors of today's Bulgarian people arrived in the Balkans in the middle of the sixth century. In the seventh century they were conquered by Turkic Bulgars whose original home was in central Asia, but the conquerors in turn were assimilated by the more numerous Slavs. Thus the First Bulgarian Empire (681–1018) by the ninth century was culturally and linguistically Slavic, making it the world's first well-organized Slavic state. During the ninth century missionaries from Constantinople converted the Bulgarians to the Orthodox version of Christianity. The missionaries also developed a Cyrillic alphabet for the Bulgarian language. Bulgarian thus became the first written Slavic language; the Bulgarians also became the first Europeans to have a written literature in a language other than Hebrew, Latin, or Greek. Their empire enjoyed a cultural golden age in the late ninth and early tenth centuries as it expanded its boundaries to include a large chunk of the Balkans. However, the empire weakened and was conquered by the Byzantine Empire early in the eleventh century. After a decisive battle in 1014, the Byzantine emperor committed one of history's more gruesome war crimes by blinding 14,000 Bulgarian soldiers.

The Bulgarians suffered under the Byzantines, but they were able to reestablish their independence and found a Second Bulgarian Empire in 1186. It lasted for slightly more than two hundred years, but like the first empire it fell to a powerful empire to the east, the Ottoman Empire. This time oppressive foreign rule, the grimmest period in Bulgarian history, lasted for five hundred years. The Ottomans taxed the Bulgarian people into poverty and stifled economic, political and social life. Rebellions were frequent and unsuccessful, and punishment severe. In the eighteenth and nineteenth centuries, as the Ottoman Empire weakened, it exploited Bulgaria even more than before. However, during the mid-1800s, the European shuffling of political power delayed Bulgaria's liberation. The Bulgarian cause was hurt during the Crimean War

(1853–1856) when Britain and France sided with Turkey against Russia order to check the growth of Russian power. Brutal Turkish repression of an uprising in 1876 shocked Western Europe. It also helped provoke yet another Russo-Turkish war, which the Russians won. The other European powers again stepped in to limit Russian power. While still denying Bulgaria full independence, the European powers made Bulgaria autonomous, or semi-independent. The European powers also denied Bulgaria the region of Macedonia, striking yet another blow against Bulgarian pride. Finally, in 1908, Bulgaria took advantage of an international crisis to declare itself fully independent. Through it all, the Bulgarians were grateful to the Russians for their help in throwing off the Turkish yoke, a gratitude that still is deeply felt today.

Bulgaria became involved in two Balkan wars, in 1912 and 1913, in an unsuccessful attempt to win Macedonia, which ended up divided between Serbia and Greece. The goal of getting Macedonia lured Bulgaria into World War I on the German, and therefore the losing, side. During the interwar period, Bulgaria underwent continual economic and political crisis. The turmoil led to what amounted to a dictatorship by the country's monarch, Tsar Boris III. Bulgaria then fought on the German side in World War II until 1944, when it was overrun by the Soviet army and it switched sides. Bulgaria did not suffer heavy damage during World War II compared with other countries, and did not have severe terms imposed on it by the victorious Allies. However, Bulgaria did pay a price because of its location. When the smoke of battle finally cleared in 1945, it was under Soviet occupation and firmly under Moscow's control.

Bulgaria Under Communism

By 1944, Bulgaria was being run by the Fatherland Front, an organization dominated by the Soviet-controlled Bulgarian Communist Party. In 1946 the Front won a rigged election and abolished the monarchy, and by 1947 Bulgaria was proclaimed a "people's republic." Its premier was Georgi Demitrov, the so-called father of Bulgarian Communism and a longtime Stalin loyalist. Five years after Demitrov's death in 1949, Todor Zhivkov became Bulgaria's Communist leader. He dominated Bulgarian politics until 1989, the year Communism collapsed in Eastern Europe. Zhivkov ran a tight Stalinist dictatorship, but still managed to make Bulgaria one of the more prosperous countries in Eastern Europe by permitting small amounts of flexibility for factory managers and farmers. At the same time, his regime followed a hard line on ethnic matters. During the mid-1980s it carried out a program of forced assimilation against both the Turkish and Pomak minorities. About 350,000 Turks emigrated to Turkey, although many later returned to Bulgaria because of difficult living conditions in Turkey.

Zhivkov managed to hang on to power through most of 1989, despite the turmoil sweeping Eastern Europe. His regime began to totter in early November, when more than nine thousand people in Sofia staged Bulgaria's first democratic protest rally since World War II. A week later, on November 10, the day after the opening of the Berlin Wall, Zhivkov's Communist colleagues removed him from office. He was replaced as party leader by Petur Mladenov, who immediately promised reforms. Another Communist official became prime minister. Although Communists still ruled in Bulgaria, the era of Communist dictatorship and Soviet domination joined Zhivkov in passing from the scene.

Post-Communist Bulgaria

Significant political changes took place in Bulgaria during the end of 1989 and beginning of 1990. The Communists who had removed Zhivkov still ran the government. However, they gave up their monopoly of power, allowed opposition political parties, and scheduled elections for a new parliament. Their promises included a pledge to end persecution of the Turkish community. Meanwhile, opposition groups multiplied. The most important was a coalition of political parties called the Union of Democratic Forces (UDF), which took shape in December. Its leader was

Zhelyu Zhelev, a respected philosopher who been an opponent of the Communist regime since the early 1970s. In February 1990, 200,000 people rallied in Sofia demanding the end of Communist rule. In April, Bulgaria's Communists renamed their party the Bulgarian Socialist Party (BSP) and called for a gradual changeover to a market economy.

The June 1990 parliamentary elections brought change, but not enough for many Bulgarians. The Bulgarian Socialist Party won a majority of the seats. It increased its appeal by ridding itself of those leaders most opposed to reform, but it also made use of its control of the media to tilt the electorate in its direction. Also, many voters feared the price increases and unemployment that rapid market reforms might bring. The Union of Democratic Forces, which charged the Socialist Party with election fraud, finished second. After the parliamentary election a series of protests and strikes forced President Mladenov to resign. Parliament then elected UDF leader Zhelev as president. He was Bulgaria's first non-Communist leader in more than forty years.

The next two years were marked by political instability, but also some progress toward democracy. There was minimal economic reform, as the population was badly divided over that issue. The economy, with the old system in decay but with nothing to replace it, went into a tailspin. Buildings, streets, and highways fell into disrepair, people waited for hours for gasoline, power often was shut off, and some essential foods had to be rationed. A reorganized BSP cabinet with a new prime minister began some modest reforms, but they solved almost no problems. Bulgaria did get a new constitution in 1991, and the government even put Zhivkov on trial for corruption. (He was convicted in 1992 and spent a brief time in prison.) In April 1992, the government passed legislation to make possible the return of property seized by the Communist regime between 1947 and 1962. Bulgaria also held both presidential and parliamentary elections in 1992. In January, Zhelev was reelected president, this time directly by the people. In

October the UDF won a narrow victory (110 seats to the Socialist Party's 94, out of a total of 240), and formed a coalition government that included the Movement for Rights and Freedoms (MRF), formed to represent Bulgaria's Turkish minority. Another milestone had been reached: the Communists (and former Communists of the Socialist Party) finally were out of power.

Over the next two years the UDF, like the Socialist Party before it, was torn by factionalism. It lost the backing of its Turkish allies, who complained of continued discrimination. The government did manage to begin a privatization program in June 1994, but the process was poorly organized and proceeded slowly. It proved impossible to find buyers for many money-losing enterprises. By the time new parliamentary elections were held in December 1994, 70 percent of Bulgarians were living at or below the poverty line. Inflation stood at 120 percent per year. Unemployment also was high. Not surprisingly, the BSF returned to power with a majority in parliament.

The next two years brought little relief from either political turmoil or economic hardship. After a brief economic upturn in 1995, when the economy grew by about 2 percent, a new crisis developed in 1996 and the economy shrank by almost 11 percent. As presidential elections approached in late 1996, the UDF rejected Zhelev and nominated Petar Stoyanov, a forty-four-year-old lawyer, as its presidential candidate. He was decisively elected in December. As he left office, Zhelev, who in 1989 was considered a hero by his people, evaluated the situation in his country without bitterness, but rather with sadness:

> These are desperate people brought to the verge of despair and violence. Their frustration is so strong because nothing is moving ahead. Their life is getting worse under these conditions of democracy.[5]

Actually, it appeared that Zhelev was speaking just as Bulgaria had hit bottom. New parliamentary elections in April 1997 gave the UDF a decisive majority in parliament. The election boosted the optimism of President Stoyanov, who told the new parliament:

> Today everyone is convinced that a new reformist government has been born in Bulgaria, and you are here in Parliament as the most important part of it.[6]

After the election President Stoyanov appointed Ivan Kostov, a confident forty-eight-year-old economist, as prime minister. The new UDF government had some success in stabilizing the economy. By the end of the year inflation stood at just one percent, food shortages were eliminated, and wages had risen slightly.

Progress continued over the next two years, as the economy grew by 3.5 percent in 1998 and by 2.5 percent in 1999. The decline from 1998 to 1999 was caused in part by the Kosovo conflict between NATO and Serbia, as the NATO bombing campaign blocked Bulgaria's transportation routes to Western Europe and therefore cut its export trade. Several errant NATO missiles also hit Bulgaria, including one that destroyed a home on the outskirts of Sofia. Although Bulgaria sided with the NATO alliance, many Bulgarians were sympathetic to the Serbs, with whom they have close religious and language ties. In any event, Bulgaria's economy picked up again after the shooting stopped. Still, as the year ended, serious economic problems remained, including an unemployment rate that rose from 12 percent in 1998 to a whopping 18 percent in 1999.

Meanwhile, a seven-story steel-and-marble building in the southwestern city of Blagoevgrad provided an upbeat message about Bulgaria's future. Once it was the headquarters of the local Communist Party. Now, as the 3-foot (0.9-meter)-high Cyrillic letters on the building's front announce, it is the "American University in Bulgaria." It accepts students who score a minimum of 1,200 out of 1,600 on American SAT exams. They study, exclusively in English, an American-style curriculum focusing on liberal arts and courses with practical business applications. Its graduates—the first class graduated in 1998—are snapped up by Bulgaria's leading businesses. As one graduate put it, "You get more than a degree; you get a life."[7] The school's goal is to help provide Bulgaria with the skilled and Western-oriented leadership it needs in the new century to make the transition to a democratic and free-market society.

Albania

Albania is unique in Europe for several reasons. It is the only country on the continent with a majority Muslim population. During the Communist era, it was the only Eastern European country that allied itself first with the Soviet Union, then with China, and then refused to have anything to do with either of the two Communist giants. Cut off from outsiders by its Communist government, Albania was Europe's most isolated country for four decades. It was the most loyal to Communism, not emerging from Communist rule until 1992, even later than Russia. Finally, Albania emerged from Communism as Europe's poorest and most economically backward country. Even today, agriculture generates more than half of Albania's economy.

Albania is an oval-shaped country with an area of 11,100 square miles (28,748 square kilometers), slightly larger than Maryland, located along the western coast of the Balkan Peninsula. Its longest border is its 220-mile (354-kilometer) coastline, about three quarters of which lies on the Adriatic Sea. The portion of Albania's coastline on the Ionian sea is a region of especially beautiful scenery known as the Riviera of Flowers. Yugoslavia surrounds Albania's northern tip on three sides. About half of that border is with the province of Kosovo, 90 percent of whose population is ethnic Albanian. Tension between Albanians and Serbs makes it one of the worst potential flash points in the Balkans.

About three quarters of Albania is mountains and rugged hills. Most of the rest is a narrow coastal plain that runs about 124 miles (200 kilometers) from north to south. It averages only about 10 miles (16 kilometers) wide, except for a section in the center of the country that reaches inland for about 31 miles (50 kilometers). The plain has generally poor soil, and contains large swampy areas. There is a second, smaller lowland broken by hills in southern Albania, opposite the island of Corfu. About one third of Albania is forest and swampland, and another third is pasture. Only about one fifth of the country is farmland. Albania has three large lakes. One of them, Lake Ohrid (shared with Macedonia), is the deepest lake in the Balkans. The country has a Mediterranean climate, with mild rainy winters and hot dry summers. In the mountains, the winters are colder, with heavy snowfall.

Albania is Europe's main producer of chromium ore, and has about 5 percent of the world's total reserves. Other important natural resources are timber, copper, and nickel. Albania

An Albanian man takes his lambs for a walk in downtown Tirana.

also has some oil and natural-gas deposits, and foreign interests are anxious to explore for more, both onshore and offshore. Major crops include wheat, corn, and a variety of vegetables. Hydroelectric dams generate about 80 percent of the country's electricity. Albania's few industries produce processed food, textiles, oil products, and cement.

About 95 percent of Albania's 3.35 million citizens are ethnic Albanians. About 3 percent are ethnic Greeks. There are also small numbers of Serbs, Gypsies, and Bulgarians. Seventy percent of the population is Muslim, 20 percent Orthodox, and 10 percent Catholic. Tirana (population 243,000) is Albania's capital and largest city. Durres (population 79,000), an ancient town on the Adriatic coast founded by the Greeks in the seventh century B.C., is the country's second-largest city and main port.

Albanian History to 1945

The Illyrians, ancestors of today's Albanians, probably arrived in the Balkans about 1000 B.C. The Greeks established colonies along parts of the Albanian coast, but an independent Illyrian kingdom existed and reached its peak in the third century B.C. By the middle of the next century, Rome controlled the region, along with the rest of the Balkans. When the Roman Empire was divided in A.D. 395, Albania became part of the Eastern Roman Empire. During the next several centuries, control over all or part of Albania passed back and forth between the Byzantines, Serbs, Bulgarians, Normans, and Venetians.

Independent local chieftains ruled Albania for a short time in the mid-1300s. However, the Ottoman conquest began in the fifteenth century and proceeded despite determined Albanian resistance. In the mid-1400s Albania's national hero, Skanderbeg, led the resistance, defeating the Ottomans in more than twenty battles. When Skanderbeg died in 1468, the Ottoman Sultan supposedly said:

> Asia and Europe are mine at last. Woe to Christendom! She has lost her sword and shield.[8]

Albania formally came under Ottoman rule in 1479; it did not regain its independence until the twentieth century. Resistance continued for much of that time, especially in the highlands, which never were fully conquered. Thousands of Albanians fled the country at various times. Most of those who stayed converted to Islam in order to escape official anti-Christian discrimination. After Albania finally achieved its independence in 1912, it was bitterly disappointed in 1913 when Europe's major powers turned Kosovo and its largely Albanian population over to Serbia, which had occupied the territory during the Second Balkan War.

Albania once again became a battleground for outside countries during World War I and was fortunate to reemerge as an independent country in 1920. However, turmoil, including foreign intervention, continued. After being declared a republic in 1925, Albania became a monarchy when its president declared himself king. Italy, under fascist dictator Benito Mussolini, invaded and occupied the county in 1939. Among the groups that fought Italian occupation was the newly founded Communist Party. It seized control of the country after the war and established a strict Communist dictatorship.

Albania Under Communism

The Communists used brute force to take control of Albania and continued to use the same measures to rule. They officially declared Albania a People's Republic in January 1946 and built a strict Stalinist dictatorship that controlled almost every aspect of the people's lives and denied them the most basic human and civil rights. Albania, fearing Yugoslavian expansion, was at first friendly with the Soviet Union. When Soviet leader Nikita Khrushchev began his reforms in the mid-1950s, Albania's long-time Communist dictator Enver Hoxha formed an alliance with the People's Republic of China. However, when China began to improve relations with the United States, Albania broke with China. Meanwhile, Hoxha maintained his personal control, assisted by his wife Nexhmije, until his death in

Enver Hoxha in 1956

1985 after a long illness. Hoxha kept Albania in almost total isolation; when he died the county had only 700 television sets and
400 cars, all in the hands of the state. The dictator was succeeded by his chief lieutenant, Ramiz Alia.

Albania 1985–1992

Although Alia continued Hoxha's policies of isolation from the
United States, the Soviet Union, and China, he also understood
that Albania badly needed reform. He increased ties with Italy
and Greece, expanded foreign trade, allowed some tourists to
visit, and eased antireligion policies. In 1990, after demonstrations in several towns, Alia began limited political reforms.
They turned out to be too little too late. In the age of modern
communications, not even Albania's Communist dictatorship
could prevent the news about the changes sweeping Eastern
Europe from reaching the people. By 1991 Alia and the Communists were losing their grip. Thousands of Albanians were

trying to leave the country; others were openly demonstrating and demanding reforms. In the spring of 1991, Albania had its first multiparty elections of the Communist era. The Communist Party won, but an opposition group called the Democratic Party of Albania (DPA) finished a strong second. After the election the Communist Party, trying to break with the past, renamed itself the Socialist Party of Albania (SPA).

It is to Alia's credit that he avoided violence and permitted change that he eventually was unable to control, even as he tried to keep his party in power. In March 1992, under a new electoral law, Albania once again elected a parliament. This time the Democratic Party won 92 of 140 seats. The Socialists won only 38 seats and Alia resigned as president. Parliament then elected to the presidency Democratic Party leader Dr. Sali Berisha, who was a cardiologist before entering politics. After forty-seven years, Communist rule in Albania was over.

Post-Communist Albania

Albania's poverty and lack of democratic traditions made its exit from Communism difficult. President Berisha was determined to rid the country of Communist officials, and between 1992 and 1994 the new government tried and imprisoned several of them—including Nexhmije Hoxha and Ramiz Alia—for crimes they committed while in office. In 1995 Ilir Hoxha, son of the former dictator, also was imprisoned after being convicted on the vague charge of inciting national hatred. Meanwhile, Berisha was behaving increasingly like a dictator. There was criticism that some of the trials of former Communists were unfair, in particular the trial of SPA leader and former prime minister Fatos Nano. International observers of the March 1996 parliamentary elections won by the DPA reported widespread fraud and intimidation of voters. Many of those activities were the work of the government's secret police.

Matters came to a head early in 1997 when several large high-risk investment schemes collapsed. Thousands of Albanians lost their life savings. Government officials were accused of being involved in the schemes and there were several violent antigovernment demonstrations. In the middle of all the turmoil, parliament reelected Berisha, who was unopposed, to a second five-year presidential term. By then protesters had armed themselves and seized control of several southern towns. They even succeeded in seizing the central jail in Tirana and freeing prisoners, including Alia and Nano (to whom Berisha later granted a pardon).

A semblance of order was restored when the Organization for Security and Cooperation in Europe (OSCE), to which fifty-four nations, including Albania, belong, stepped in. It brought Albania's political leaders together and got them to agree to new elections. The OSCE then sent a military force of seven thousand to Albania. It was accompanied by five hundred international monitors whose job it was to monitor new parliamentary elections. The elections took place in June. This time it was the Democratic Party that paid the price for economic hard times and authoritarian behavior. The Socialists won 101 out of 155 seats, the Democratic Party only 27. Berisha hung on to office for three weeks before bowing to pressure from both home and abroad and resigning. The parliament then elected Rexhep Mejdani, a fifty-three-year-old physicist and Socialist Party official, as Albania's president in a vote the Democratic Party boycotted. Mejdani appointed Nano, who had only recently been in prison, as prime minister.

Notwithstanding his party's deep roots in totalitarian Communism, Mejdani sounded much more like a traditional Western European social democrat when he spoke about his main goal:

> I feel a deep responsibility for the office I now hold. This country needs peace and love instead of dividing people.[9]

He had a huge job on his hands. Albania did take a political step forward in November 1998 when voters approved the new constitution. That was followed by a severe economic blow. During the Kosovo crisis and NATO bombing campaign against Serbia of March-June 1999, more than half a million refugees driven from their homes by Serbia poured into Albania. Caring for them cost the government several hundred million dollars, an enormous burden in a country where the average government employee had a monthly salary of $71.

Albania's long-term problems are daunting. Large parts of the country remain outside effective government control. In the countryside entire towns are controlled by heavily armed gangs or warlords whose main occupation is smuggling. There are an estimated 650,000 modern weapons, mainly the famous Soviet Kalashnikov assault rifles, in the country, one for every six Albanian man, woman, and child. Perhaps even more troubling than the gangs is Albania's old tradition of clan and regional feuds. They have disrupted the country for centuries, regardless of what government ruled in Tirana. One particularly devastating feud reportedly lasted for 240 years. It was with these heavy burdens, and more, that Albania began the year 2000.

Chapter Six

The Former Yugoslavia

There are few places in the world with ethnic problems as complicated and tragic as the scenic country once known as Yugoslavia, the "land of the South Slavs." Six nationalities traditionally have been identified as South Slavs: Serbs, Croats, Montenegrins, Slovenes, Macedonians, and Bulgarians. They are defined by the closely related languages they speak. Language, however, is not the only factor determining each individual South Slav nationality. The Serbs and Croats speak Serbo-Croatian, for example, but are divided by religion, the Serbs being Eastern Orthodox and the Croatians Roman Catholic. The Montenegrins really are Serbs. They have a distinct identity, however, because for centuries their fierce resistance kept their mountain stronghold independent of the Ottoman Empire. The Macedonians have a problem with recognition. The Bulgarians insist they are Bulgarian, while some Serb nationalists call them "South Serbs."

Before the creation of Yugoslavia, the individual South Slav groups, despite their common origins, all had distinct histories. From the start, this made the task of melding five of them (the Bulgarians were left out of Yugoslavia) into a single nation a high-risk project at best. The job was further complicated by the presence of what some consider another South Slav group, the Bosnians (or Bosniaks). The Bosnians actually are primarily descendants of Serbs or Croats who converted to Islam after the Ottoman conquest. This additional religious factor created a triangular relationship of mutual suspicion and hostility in areas where the three groups lived. Yugoslavia also included a large community of non-Slavic Albanians, as well as smaller numbers of other non-Slavic groups. The unstable multicultural structure that was Yugoslavia was first hammered together in 1918. In 1991 it shattered in a violent outburst of ethnic hatred, religious intolerance, and political opportunism.

The South Slavs of Yugoslavia to 1918

The Slavic tribes that over time evolved into the South Slavs first arrived in the Balkan Peninsula during the sixth century. Precisely where they came from is uncertain; most scholars believe their original homeland was in Ukraine. Whatever their origins, unlike earlier invaders, such as the Huns and Goths, who passed through the region, the Slavs had come to the Balkans to stay.

The Serbs

The Serbs settled in territory controlled by the Byzantine Empire. Late in the ninth century they converted to the Byzantine Eastern Orthodox version of Christianity. The Serbs lived under Byzantine rule until they established an independent kingdom in the twelfth century. The early thirteenth century saw the first works of Serbian literature. Serbia reached the peak of its power in the fourteenth century, when under Stefan Dusan (1346–1355) it dominated much of the Balkan Peninsula. Many monasteries were built during this Serbian "golden age." However, that age was short-lived. In 1389 the Serbs lost the hard-fought Battle of Kosovo Polje (Kosovo Field, or "field of the black birds") to the invading Ottoman Turks. Although the Turks did not actually occupy Serbia until the fifteenth century, the defeat in 1389 was decisive and marked the beginning of five hundred bitter years of Turkish rule. To this day the Serbian heroic songs and epic poems recall and mourn the disaster that befell the nation at Kosovo.

No Balkan people suffered more under Turkish rule than the Serbs, whose rebellions and defiance were met by savage Turkish repression. Serbia secured its freedom in several stages as the Ottoman Empire weakened during the nineteenth century, finally winning full independence in 1878. During the years before World War I, Serbia was an active player in Balkan territorial disputes. It lost out to Austria-Hungary in 1908 for control of Bosnia-Herzegovena, but won a large slice of Ottoman territory after the two Balkan Wars of 1912–1913. Serbia was at the center of the crisis that sparked World War I; it fought on the Allied side and suffered terribly before victory came in 1918.

The Croats

The Croats arrived in the Balkans along with the Serbs, but thereafter their histories diverged. The Croats accepted the Roman Catholic version of Christianity after being conquered in the ninth century by Charlemagne, emperor of the Franks. They established an independent kingdom that lasted from the early tenth to the late eleventh century, but then fell under Hungarian rule. In the wake of Hungary's defeat by the Turks at the Battle of Mohacs in 1526, Croatia was divided between the Austrian and Ottoman empires until the Austrians drove the Turks from the region in the 1690s. Croatia enjoyed a cultural revival in the nineteenth century, but remained part of Austria-Hungary until that empire collapsed in 1918 after its defeat in World War I.

In short, while the Serbs were Eastern Orthodox and spent five hundred years under Ottoman rule, the Croats were Roman

Catholics and were ruled largely by Hungarians and Germans. Through it all, the Croats saw themselves as representatives of Western civilization in the Balkans and often looked down on the Serbs and other Balkan Slavs as culturally backward and followers of the wrong form of Christianity. The Serbs in turn viewed the Croats as a threat because of their ties to the Roman Catholic Church and the Germans of Austria-Hungary.

The Slovenes

More than any other South Slavic group, the Slovenes' history has been oriented westward. The westward pull began in the eighth century when the Slovenes were conquered by the Franks, who also converted them to Christianity. In the ninth century Slovenia became part of the German-dominated Holy Roman Empire, and in the fourteenth century it fell under Hapsburg control. Slovenia remained under German rule, except for a few years of French rule during the Napoleonic era, until Austria-Hungary collapsed in 1918. The era of French rule was important because French ideas about democracy and nationalism influenced Slovenian intellectuals. The French also promoted the concept of South Slav unity, which later evolved into the idea of an independent Yugoslavia.

The Montenegrins

The Montenegrins exist as a separate nationality because a small group of Serbs, high in their mountain home near the Adriatic Sea, held off the Turks for five hundred years. It became a refuge for Serbs fleeing Turkish rule. As they battled the Turks century after century, the Montenegrins sometimes lost battles and some territory, but never were conquered. They developed a unique form of government led by elected prince-bishops called *vladike*. That form of rule lasted until reforms in 1852 made the monarchy a strictly secular institution. Although the Turkish sultan recognized Montenegro's independence as early as 1799, formal independence did not come until the Congress of Berlin in 1878. At that time Montenegro received some additional territory that included an outlet to the Adriatic Sea.

The Macedonians

In ancient times Macedonia was part of the Greek world and the home of Alexander the Great. Today's Macedonians are descendants of Slavic tribes that arrived in the seventh century. Since then Macedonia was always controlled by foreigners, whether Byzantines, Bulgarians, Serbs, or Turks. The Turks, during more than five centuries of control, destroyed the old Macedonian aristocracy and enserfed the Christian peasants who worked on large Turkish-owned estates. European power politics enabled Turkey to hold on to Macedonia until the twentieth century. In 1902 and 1903, the Turks brutally crushed Macedonian uprisings. The two Balkan wars of 1912–1913 finally broke the Turkish grip on Macedonia; in the Second Balkan War, Greece and Serbia defeated Bulgaria and divided most of Macedonia between themselves. Bulgaria to this day has not accepted its loss of the region.

The Bosnians

The region that became Bosnia-Herzegovena (hereafter called Bosnia) was settled by Serbs and Croats in the seventh century. It was controlled by a variety of powers before achieving independence in the twelfth century. At that time many Bosnian nobles rejected both the Catholic and Eastern Orthodox faiths and adopted Bogomilism, a form of Christianity considered a heresy by both churches. After periods of weakness and Hungarian control, an independent Bosnia reached its peak in the mid-fourteenth century. The Turks conquered the region in the fifteenth century. At that point, mainly to keep their land and privileges, most of the Bosnian nobles abandoned Bogomilism and accepted Islam. The region remained under Turkish rule until 1878, when, despite Serb objections, the

Congress of Berlin placed it under Austrian-Hungarian occupation. In 1908 Austria-Hungary infuriated Serbia by formally annexing Bosnia. Continued tensions over the region provoked the assassination of the heir to the Austrian throne by a Serbian terrorist in Sarajevo, Bosnia's capital, in August 1914. It was the spark that ignited World War I.

Yugoslavia, 1918–1945

The idea for a state to unite the South Slavs took shape during World War I when Serb and Croat representatives met in 1917 on the Mediterranean island of Corfu. Although the Serbs and Croats disagreed on many issues, they did agree on a Yugoslav state under the ruling Serbian dynasty. In December 1918 they established the "Kingdom of Serbs, Croats, and Slovenes." It consisted of Serbia, Montenegro, and South Slavic territory—including Croatia, Slovenia, and Bosnia—that formerly belonged to the collapsed Austrian-Hungarian Empire. In 1929 its name was officially changed to the Kingdom of Yugoslavia.

The Yugoslav state was badly fragmented along ethnic lines and lacked an ethnic majority. Its population was about 43 percent Serb (and Montenegrin), 23 percent Croat, 8.5 percent Slovene, 5 percent Macedonian, and 6 percent Bosnian. The remainder consisted of non-Slavic minorities, including Albanians, Hungarians, Greeks, Bulgarians, and Romanians. Despite the hopes of its founders, Yugoslavia from the start was plagued by ethnic conflicts. The most serious was between the Serbs and Croats over the issue of autonomy; the Serbs wanted a strong central government while the Croats demanded regional autonomy. By 1929 Yugoslavia was a dictatorship under its Serbian king. That dictatorship remained in place despite the king's assassination in 1934 by Croat extremists. An attempt to increase internal stability in 1939 by granting the Croats autonomy solved little. Other ethnic groups immediately demanded similar concessions, and nationalistic Serbs bitterly opposed the agreement. Meanwhile, in September 1939 Nazi Germany dragged Europe into World War II. When Yugoslavia sided with Germany in 1941, anti-German forces overthrew the government. The new government proclaimed Yugoslavia's neutrality. The Germans then invaded, adding the horrors of Nazism and war to Yugoslavia's other troubles.

Germany and its Italian, Hungarian, and Bulgarian allies all took pieces of Yugoslav territory, and the German army occupied Serbia. In Croatia, enlarged to include Bosnia, Nazi Germany found enthusiastic allies in the fascist and anti-Semitic Ustashe movement. The Nazis put the Ustashe in power as its puppet to govern a supposedly independent Croatia. The Ustashe then waged a campaign of genocide that wiped out most of the Jewish population of Croatia and Bosnia. Thousands of Gypsies also were murdered. However, the main Ustashe target was the 1.9 million Serbs living in territory it controlled. The Serbs became the object of a campaign that later would be given the name "ethnic cleansing." The Ustashe murdered at least 200,000 Serbs, and probably many more. It also carried out a program of forced conversion to Catholicism. In Bosnia the Ustashe was aided by local Muslim collaborators, more than 20,000 of whom enlisted in a military unit of the SS, the most fearsome branch of the Nazi German regime. The single most important Ustashe killing ground was the infamous Jasenovac concentration camp on the Sava River near the Bosnian border. The victims included Jews and Gypsies, but most were Serbs.

Two organizations resisted the Germans and their Yugoslav collaborators: the conservative Yugoslav Army of the Fatherland ("Chetniks"), led by General Draza Mihajlović, and the Communist Party of Yugoslavia ("Partisans"), led by Josep Broz Tito. The two groups themselves were enemies and fought each other in what amounted to a civil war within the larger war against the Germans. In the end, Tito's partisans proved more effective in fighting the Germans and won Allied support. His group also received Soviet support, especially after the Soviet army occupied eastern Yugoslavia in late 1944. Tito then brutally suppressed any opposition to Communist rule, killing thousands in the process. By late 1945 the Communist Party had established a dictatorship over Yugoslavia.

Yugoslavia Under Communism: The Tito Era

Tito dominated Yugoslavia until his death. In large part because of Tito, Yugoslavia was unique among the Communist states in Eastern Europe in that it was genuinely independent of Soviet control. Tito's split with Stalin in 1948 permanently shattered the unity of the Communist world (see chapter 1). After 1948, Yugoslavia took a neutral position in the Cold War between the United States and the Soviet Union. Tito's policies at home further distinguished Yugoslavia from its Communist neighbors. A new constitution in 1946 divided the country into six republics: Serbia, Montenegro, Croatia, Slovenia, Macedonia, and Bosnia. Each republic had some autonomy, although real power remained in the hands of Tito and the Communist Party leadership. Serbia also contained two autonomous regions: Kosovo in the south, where the majority of the population was Albanian; and Vojvodina in the north, where about a quarter of the population was Hungarian. Tito's policy of "national Communism," introduced in the early 1950s, ended collectivization and allowed factories a measure of self-management. The Yugoslav people were allowed far more freedom than existed in any other Communist state.

However, although ethnic tensions were suppressed under Tito's powerful leadership, they were not solved. In addition, by the 1970s the Yugoslav economy, despite Tito's innovations, was running into serious problems. Nor did Tito, always suspicious of any potential rivals, prepare the Yugoslavia's political system for the inevitable post-Tito era. When he died in 1980 Yugoslavia's buried but unsolved problems began to undermine the unity he had tried to build.

The Decline and Disintegration of Communist Yugoslavia

The post-Tito era began badly. The new nine-man rotating presidency, which Tito had created to take over after his death, did not work. It could not cope with the upsurge of openly expressed ethnic tensions. Ethnic trouble began in 1981 with Albanian demonstrations and riots in Serbia's Kosovo region. Although Kosovo was of enormous historic importance to the Serbs, by the 1980s Albanians accounted for almost 90 percent of its population. In 1974 Tito had expanded its autonomy. During the 1981 disorders several people were killed and more than 20,000 Serbs and Montenegrins fled Kosovo. There was more trouble in 1987 when thousands of Serbs and Montenegrins came to Kosovo from Serbia to stage their own demonstration. In 1987 Slobodan Milosevic, a militant and ruthless Serbian nationalist, became Serbian Communist Party leader. His inflammatory talk about annexing parts of Croatia, Macedonia, and Bosnia to create a "Greater Serbia" alarmed leaders of those republics. In 1989 Milosevic revoked Kosovo's autonomy and sent troops to that region to suppress Albanian protests. Meanwhile, economic reforms introduced in 1988 to revive the economy led to higher prices for many goods, which in turn led to strikes and protests by workers.

By 1990, a small civil war was smoldering in Kosovo. Meanwhile, the winds of change that had swept away the Communist regimes in the former Soviet satellites had reached Yugoslavia. In the elections held in Yugoslavia's six republics over the course of the year, only Serbia and Montenegro kept the Communists in office. While Milosevic was reelected president in Serbia, a nationalist named Franjo Tudjman, a politician openly sympathetic to Croatia's wartime Ustashe regime, won the presidency of Croatia. In the fall, both Croatia and Slovenia suggested transforming Yugoslavia into a loose confederation in which each member state in effect would be independent. Macedonia and Bosnia supported an even looser structure. A series of negotiations produced no agreement, and in June 1991 Croatia and Slovenia declared their independence from Yugoslavia.

The Serbs, who controlled the Yugoslav army, responded with force, at least in Croatia. The fighting in Slovenia, which lasted ten days, actually was provoked by the Slovenians. They more than held their own in battles with largely Serb Yugoslav troops who often did not understand why the Slovenians suddenly were their enemies. Fighting in Croatia continued even after negotiations produced an agreement in which both Croatia and Slovenia postponed their secession for three months. By September, the same month that Macedonia declared independence, the Serbs controlled one third of Croatia. In October, the same month that Bosnia seceded, Croatia and Slovenia put their secession in effect. Both the United Nations and the European Community became involved in the effort to restore peace.

When the smoke finally cleared in late 1991 and early 1992, Yugoslavia was no more. In its place were five independent countries: Croatia, Macedonia, Slovenia, Bosnia, and a shrunken Yugoslavia consisting of Serbia and Montenegro. Thousands of people already had been killed in the fighting and perhaps a million people were homeless, but in fact the fighting had just begun. Despite the presence of a United Nations peacekeeping force in Croatia (UNPROFOR), the Serbs still controlled about 30 percent of the country, mainly Serb-populated areas. In Bosnia, where a plurality (about 44 percent) of the population was Muslim, both Serbs and Croats each were taking control of areas where they had large populations. The death of Yugoslavia was giving birth to the worst European conflict since World War II.

Slovenia Since Independence

Slovenia is a country of about 2 million people in the northwest corner of the Balkan Peninsula. With an area of about 7,819 square miles (20,252 square kilometers), about the size of New

Jersey, it is the smallest country in Eastern Europe. Slovenia is a largely mountainous country on the southern, or "sunny" side, of the Alps, the great mountain range of south-central Europe. The only exception is a lowland region near the Adriatic coast. Slovenia's coastal region has a Mediterranean climate; farther east and inland the climate becomes continental with cold winters and mild to hot summers. The country is drained by two of the Danube's important tributaries, the Drava in the east and the Sava in the center of the country. Mount Triglav in the Julian Alps along the Italian border, at 9,400 feet (2,864 meters), is Slovenia's highest peak. The Triglav National Park just south of the mountain is famous for its many species of flowering plants.

Slovenia was the most industrialized, urbanized, and prosperous of the former Yugoslav republics and today has the highest standard of living in Eastern Europe. Its most important natural resources, aside from wood, are coal, lead, zinc, mercury, uranium, and silver. Much of Slovenia's industrial out-

The mountains push right up against the sea along the beautiful Adriatic coastline.

put is based on its mineral resources. The country also produces electronics, home appliances, trucks, textiles, and wood products. Its forests, which cover half the country, are home to 2,900 plant species and shelter large populations of deer, boar, and other animals. Beneath a limestone plateau in Slovenia's southwestern Karst region is a huge network of caves, the largest of its kind in Europe. Similar caves elsewhere in the world are called "karst" caves. Slovenia's largest city and capital is Ljubljana, which means "beloved" in Slovenian. Ethnic Slovenians make up about 90 percent of the country's population. Croats and Serbs are the largest minorities. More than 95 percent of the people are Roman Catholics.

Slovenia began its independence with a leadership elected in 1990. Its prime minister, Lojze Peterle, headed the Slovenian Christian Democrats, one of the non-Communist parties that together formed a majority coalition in parliament. The president, chosen by parliament, was Milan Kucan, leader of the Party of Democratic Reform, the reorganized and renamed former Communist party.

Slovenians, given their historic links with Austria and their location on the western edge of the Balkans, usually stressed their ties to Central Europe rather than to Yugoslavia. Thus they focused on expanding rail and road links with Austria and Hungary, while doing nothing to improve the rutted asphalt strip that barely served as a road to Zagreb, Croatia's capital. Also, geography favored the Slovenes. Because Croatia stood between Slovenia and the rest of Yugoslavia, the Slovenes were sheltered from Yugoslavia's various military conflicts, particularly the civil war that raged in Bosnia after 1992 (see the Bosnia section below). Still, Slovenia did get involved in the Bosnian war, and in an embarrassing manner. In mid-1993 it was discovered that highly placed Slovenian government officials, in violation of a UN embargo on arms shipments to the former Yugoslavia, were selling arms to Bosnian Muslim forces and to Croatia. This discovery caused a major political scandal.

Although Slovenian political life had some difficult moments after 1991, as a whole democratic institutions took root there better than elsewhere in the Balkans. The country adopted a new constitution in 1991. In December 1992 Slovenia held parliamentary and presidential elections. The Liberal Democratic Party, one of the non-Communist groups that joined together to defeat the Communists in 1990, won the most seats. Its leader, Dr. Janez Drnovsek, who had been prime minister since April, thus continued to hold that position. The voters, casting their ballots directly for their president for the first time, reelected Milan Kucan to that largely ceremonial post; and they voted him into office again in 1997.

Slovenia's economy meanwhile performed reasonably well. Beginning in 1994 the economy grew between 3 and 5 percent per year. The gradual pace of economic reform allowed Slovenia to avoid some of the hardships experienced elsewhere in the former Communist world. By 1998 half the economy was in private hands. The main problem was the slow start in privatizing state-owned industries. Slovenia nonetheless was one of four Eastern European countries (the others were Poland, Hungary, and the Czech Republic) invited to discuss joining the European Union. Whereas in 1991 two thirds of Slovenia's trade was with the other Yugoslav republics, by mid-1999 Slovenia was trading mainly with its European neighbors to the west and north. The Slovenians were achieving their goal of "rejoining" Central Europe, although not quickly enough for some of them. As one foreign ministry official put it:

> Look what is happening in the former Yugoslavia. The conflict is not over. the economies are a disaster, and there is no real democratic rule. Can you blame us for wanting to cut our ties as fast as we can?[1]

In any event, as of the late 1990s, the former Yugoslavia's smallest successor state was its biggest success story.

Macedonia Since Independence

Macedonia is a rectangular country of about 2.2 million people squeezed into the middle of the Balkan Peninsula without access to the sea. Its area of 9,928 square miles (25,713 square kilometers) makes it slightly larger than Vermont. A large part of the country is a rugged plateau between 2,000 and 3,000 feet (600 and 900 meters) high. Most of the rest is mountainous. The main exception is the valley of the Vandar River, which bisects the country as it flows from northwest to southeast before crossing into Greece. Two large and shimmering Balkan jewels, Lakes Ohrid (shared with Albania) and Prespa (shared with Albania and Greece), lie partially within Macedonia. Lake Ohrid is 965 feet (294 meters) deep—the deepest lake in the Balkans and one of the oldest lakes in the world. Macedonia's climate is continental, except in the Vandar River valley, which enjoys a Mediterranean climate. The country has significant mineral resources, including lead, zinc, copper, and chromium. Macedonia's fertile soils produce a large variety of vegetables, grains, and fruits, some of which are exported. Macedonia also produces some of the world's finest tobacco. Major industries produce metals, textiles, chemicals, and cigarettes.

Skopje, on the banks of the Vandar River, is Macedonia's capital and largest city. Ethnic Macedonians make up about two thirds of the country's population. Albanians account for 22 percent, and that percentage is increasing because of a high birthrate. The ethnic tension between Macedonians and Albanians is Macedonia's most serious domestic problem, one that could threaten its territorial integrity. Other minorities include Turks, Serbs, and Gypsies. About 67 percent of the population are Eastern Orthodox Christians; most of the rest, including most Albanians, are Muslims.

Macedonia's defection from Yugoslavia was a surprise. The reorganized former Communists were expected to win the fall

1990 parliamentary elections, but a coalition of nationalist groups won instead. In January 1991 Kiro Gligorov, a moderate and capable politician, was elected as the country's president. The nationalists then moved the country toward secession, which took place in the fall of 1991. A key factor in that decision was the secession of Slovenia and Croatia, which left many Macedonians worried about remaining in a smaller, Serb-dominated Yugoslavia.

Macedonia began its existence as an independent state with enormous problems. It was the poorest part of the former Yugoslavia and was torn by dangerous domestic ethnic tensions. It could not avoid feeling the impact of the civil war going on in nearby Bosnia. And it faced hostility or threats from several of its neighbors, especially Greece, but also Bulgaria, Albania, and Serbia.

The strife in Bosnia and the hostility from Greece combined to make Macedonia even poorer than before. United Nations sanctions banned trade with Serbia for its actions in the Bosnian civil war and seriously hurt the Macedonian economy. Even worse was an economic blockade by Greece that began in 1994. By 1995, percapita income in Macedonia had fallen from its 1991 level of $1,800 to $760. Unemployment reached 30 percent. Industrial production was half of its 1990 level.

Greece's hostility, which included lobbying the countries of the European Union not to recognize Macedonia as an independent country, was as hysterical as it was mean-spirited. The Greek government objected to its northern neighbor's choice of the name "Macedonia" because it supposedly meant that Skopje was laying claim to a large part of northern Greece that was part of historic Macedonia. Greece even objected to the original Macedonian flag, which included an ancient symbol the Greeks claimed as their own. As a result of Greece's diplomatic efforts, Macedonia's admission to the UN was delayed until 1993, and it was only admitted when it temporarily agreed to call itself the "Former Yugoslav Republic of Macedonia." Angered when the European Union nations and the United States finally recognized Macedonia, Greece began its economic blockade in 1994. After lengthy negotiations Macedonia agreed to change its flag and several clauses in its constitution; in October 1995 Greece ended its blockade. However, the disagreement over the name "Macedonia" continued. Meanwhile, while Bulgaria recognized Macedonia's independence, it still insisted there was no Macedonian ethnic identity or language separate from Bulgarian. Perhaps the most reassuring act by a foreign country in the early 1990s occurred in June 1993 when the United States, under UN auspices, sent five hundred marines to guard Macedonia's border with Serbia's province of Kosovo. The dual goal was to stop the fighting in Bosnia from reaching Macedonia and to protect its territory from its neighbors.

Macedonia's internal ethnic problems were even more serious than its external ones. The Albanian minority became increasingly assertive in their actions and demands. Those actions included stockpiling weapons and forming paramilitary groups. A major Albanian demand was to have a strictly Albanian-language university, which the community went ahead and established in 1995 without government permission. Extremists in both the Albanian and Macedonian communities made it increasingly difficult for the government to find workable compromises. Overall political tensions were aggravated in October 1995 when President Gligorov was severely injured in an assassination attempt.

Macedonia did manage to hold both parliamentary and presidential elections in October 1994, although claims of fraud were supported by international observers. The Alliance for Macedonia party, the former Communist group, won the election. Gligorov, who had genuine popular support, was reelected president with 78 percent of the vote.

Perhaps most remarkable, the last years of the 1990s saw a small measure of progress in Macedonia's ethnic relations. The first positive step came after the fall 1998 parliamentary election. The leading vote getter was the Internal Macedonian Revolutionary Organization (IMRO), a nationalist group that had been hostile to Macedonia's Albanian minority. After putting together a governing coalition, the party's leader, thirty-two-year-old Ljubco Grigorievski, surprised virtually everyone by inviting the leading Albanian political party to join the coalition. The new government, with Grigorievski as prime minister, took office in December. In December 1999, the IMRO's candidate, Boris Trajkovski, won Macedonia's presidential election with crucial Albanian support. In a county in which two thirds of the population was Orthodox Christian and the largest minority was Muslim, Trajkovski, an ethnic Macedonian, was a Methodist preacher trained in Kentucky. He will need all his skills as a communicator to continue the very difficult job of pulling an ethnically and religiously divided Macedonia together. Despite a few bright spots, it remains a country whose future is cloudy at best.

Bosnia-Herzegovina Since Independence

Bosnia is a wedge-shaped mountainous country in the western part of the Balkan Peninsula with an area of 19,741 square miles (51,129 square kilometers), slightly larger than Tennessee. Depending on one's point of view, Bosnia is a wedge that juts into Croatia, or Croatia forms a huge jaw that almost envelopes Bosnia. Bosnia has a generally continental climate of cold winters and hot summers. In the higher mountains—Bosnia has more than thirty peaks between 5,500 and 7,900 feet (1,700 and 2,400 meters) in height—the winters are especially long and cold and the summers short and mild. More than a third of the country is covered by forest and woodland. Bosnia's natural resources include timber, coal, iron, and other minerals. Among its major crops are wheat, corn, potatoes, tobacco, olives, wine grapes, and plums. Major industries include timber and wood products, steel, cement, cotton fabrics, and cars.

The most important thing about post-independence Bosnia is the ethnic composition of its 4.6 million people. Bosnia lacks an ethnic majority, and in recent years its major ethnic groups—Muslims or Bosniaks (44 percent), Serbs (31 percent), and Croats (17 percent)—have behaved as bitter enemies rather than as citizens of the same country. The three groups are divided primarily by religion. The Muslims are mainly the descendants of Serbs or Croats who accepted Islam after the Turkish conquest, while the Serbs are Eastern Orthodox and the Croats Roman Catholic. In fact, there is no such thing as a "Bosnian" national feeling to unite the three groups. For example, local writers tend to see themselves as Serbs or Croats. Most Bosnian Serbs would rather be part of Serbia, and most Bosnian Croats identify with Croatia. Muslims meanwhile view themselves as a distinct ethnic group linked to the Turkish and Arabic cultural traditions. As Communism dissolved, the major political parties that emerged in Bosnia were ethnically based, one each for the Muslims, Serbs, and Croats. There was no significant political party that united large numbers of people from the three mutually suspicious communities. Sarajevo (population 526,000), the country's largest city and official capital, lost most of its Serbian and Croatian population in the wake of Bosnia's civil war. By 1999 it was 90 percent Muslim, and most of the streets that once had Serbian or Croatian names had Muslim ones.

The Bosnian Civil War

The collapse of multiethnic Yugoslavia tore away the bonds that held together multiethnic Bosnia. Bosnia's history since independence has consisted mainly of a civil war from 1992 to 1995 followed by a largely futile attempt by the United Nations and NATO to create a united country. Authoritarian Serbian and Croatian political leaders, left over from the Communist era, exploited and inflamed intergroup tensions to maintain their own power, making that job more difficult. Only Alija Izetbegovic, the leader of the Bosnian Muslims and Bosnia's president after elections in 1990, had a long history of opposition to Communism before 1990. However, his writings about how to create an Islamic state and decades-long associations with Islamic fundamentalism frightened Serb and Croatian nationalists. They had no trouble using Izetbegovic's writings to convince the Serb and Croat communities they had no future in an independent Bosnia.

The civil war itself was a three-sided affair, made more complicated and deadly because the three protagonists did not always line up in the same way. The main struggle pitted the Bosnian Serbs (backed by Serbia) against both the Bosnian Croats (backed by Croatia) and the Muslims. However, during 1993 and 1994 the Croats turned against the Muslims and at times even cooperated with their bitter enemies, the Serbs. In the center of the fray, trying to end the fighting and ease the suffering, were the United Nations and NATO—the UN with peacekeeping forces and humanitarian aid and NATO with air power, which it used against the Serbs. Between 1992 and 1995 there were many cease-fires, all broken, and a series of proposed peace agreements, all of which collapsed before they could be implemented. There also were massacres of civilians and war prisoners, as well as deliberate expulsions of entire communities from their homes, a policy known as "ethnic cleansing." The Serbs, who held the advantage for most of the war, committed most of these crimes, including the worst single massacre in July 1995 in the city of Srebrenica, where they murdered more than seven thousand Muslims. But all sides committed their share of crimes. For example, on January 7, 1993, Christmas on the Eastern Orthodox calendar, Muslim soldiers from Srebrenica massacred Serbs in the nearby village of Kravica. Two months later, Croat militiamen murdered dozens of Muslims, including women, children, and elderly, in two villages northwest of Sarajevo. The list goes on. Altogether, about three quarters of the individuals accused of war crimes were Serbs; the rest were Croats or Muslims. Not until sustained NATO air strikes tipped the military balance against the Serbs was an agreement finally reached that actually stopped the fighting.

What were the goals of each side? The Muslim Bosnians declared independence to avoid having to live in a Serb-dominated country, which is what Yugoslavia became after Croatia and Slovenia seceded. They wanted Bosnia to have a relatively centralized government, as opposed to one that granted wide local autonomy. The Serb goal was the mirror opposite of the Muslim objective. Bosnia's Serbs had bitterly opposed secession from Yugoslavia, a step engineered by the Croat and Muslim leaderships. The Serbs, who had not forgotten what happened to them in World War II at the hands of the Croats and Muslims, were determined to prevent the establishment of an independent Bosnia in which they would be a minority. They wanted to clear Serb areas in Bosnia of Croat or Muslim inhabitants so those areas could join together and become part of Serbia. That was why the Serbs engaged in the brutal policy of "ethnic cleansing" that created a massive refugee problem. Ethnic cleansing involved vicious crimes, including murder, rape, and the herding of people into concentration camps. Among the Bosnian Serbs the United Nations has accused of war crimes were their leader, Dr. Radovan Karadzic, and their top military commander, Ratko Mladic. The Bosnian Serbs depended on the backing of Serbian president Slobodan Milosevic, although at times they refused to follow his orders.

The Bosnian Croat agenda was set by Croatian president Franjo Tudjman. He operated as ruthlessly as Karadzic or Milosevic, but did so according to the opportunities that presented themselves. Tudjman was prepared to cooperate with Milosevic in carving up Bosnia, apparently his original goal, if the international community permitted it. If not, Tudjman was ready to turn on the Serbs, carry out his own policy of ethnic cleansing against them (and against Muslims), and seize whatever advantage he could.

During 1992 both the Serbs and the Croats announced the establishment of their own independent "republics" in Bosnia.

By the time the UN and NATO finally were able to end the fighting in Bosnia three years later, more than 200,000 people were dead and at least 2 million, close to half the population, were refugees. The Dayton Accords of December 1995, named after the United States city where they were signed, officially preserved a "united" Bosnia. That claim was a fiction. The agreement divided Bosnia into two "entities," a Serb republic that controlled 49 percent of Bosnia and a Muslim/Croat federation that controlled 51 percent. Even the Muslim/Croat "federation" was a fiction. Mostar, its "capital," was a rigidly divided city whose Croat and Muslim inhabitants did not mix. In reality, by 1997 it was clear that Croatia, in violation of the Dayton agreement, had in practice annexed the Croat regions of the "federation." The local people carried Croatian passports, voted in Croatian elections, put Croatian license plates on their cars, and used Croatian money. The Serbs also in effect turned their republic into a separate state. NATO pressure had succeeded in forcing Karadzic from office in 1996, but his successor, Dr. Biljina Plavsic, was a militant Serb nationalist who differed from Karadzic mainly by being more flexible and diplomatic when it came to dealing with the Western powers. The problem was that elections in 1997 for the Serb republic's national assembly demonstrated that Plavsic, notwithstanding European and American support and Karadzic's documented corruption, had less support among Bosian Serbs than her rival. Making matters worse, in 1998 Plavsic was defeated in her reelection campaign by an ultra hard-line Serb nationalist.

Very few refugees—Serb, Croatian, or Muslim—dared to return to homes in regions where they would be part of the minority. Sarajevo, Bosnia's "capital," became a Muslim city to which Serbs and Croats who had fled their homes could not return. By 1996 almost all the Serbian or Croatian street names had been changed to Muslim names. The Bosnian government under President Izetbegovic, aided by several Islamic countries including Iran, was building a strictly Muslim army to defend the 30 percent of Bosnia it controlled. In general, it clearly was sympathetic to the Islamization of life in Bosnia's Muslim community. Meanwhile, years of postwar turmoil had made Bosnia the poorest part of the former Yugoslavia. By 1998 observers were asking what would happen when NATO's 35,000 peacekeeping soldiers left Bosnia alone. As one European diplomat put it:

> The force and will to build Bosnia as one nation simply do not exist. We are stuck in a holding pattern from which we cannot escape.[2]

Nor did the situation improve significantly over the next two years. In August 1999 the international agency charged with carrying out civilian aspects of the Dayton peace accords reported that hundreds of millions of dollars of foreign aid and local funds had been stolen by local officials. The corruption was across the board; those implicated included Muslim, Serb, and Croat officials. The following April, in the first elections of the new century, Serb and Croat voters casting ballots for city and town officials once again supported militant nationalist parties. Bosnia remained quiet because it was occupied by 34,000 NATO troops, including 7,500 United States soldiers that cost Washington $2 billion per year. But nowhere in Eastern Europe, except possibly in Kosovo, were the prospects for the future so bleak.

Croatia Since Independence

Croatia is a country of 21,829 square miles (56,538 square kilometers) shaped like a boomerang on the western part of the Balkan Peninsula. It was, after Serbia, the second-largest republic in the former Yugoslavia, and also, after Slovenia, the second most industrialized and prosperous. Croatia's long, jagged Adriatic coastline—about 375 miles (600 kilometers) as the crow flies, but actually 1,102 miles (1,778 kilometers) in length—forms its western border. A 12-mile (19-kilometer) wedge of Bosnia along the Adriatic coast separates the bulk of Croatia from a small strip of the country that includes

Dubrovnik, a proud independent city-state in medieval times and a major tourist attraction in modern times. Dubrovnik, the picturesque "pearl of the Adriatic," is one of several important seaports on the Croatian coast.

Croatia's rugged coastline is dominated by the Dinaric Alps mountain range. Many of its almost 1,200 offshore islands are barren rocks with mountains that drop spectacularly into the sea. Not far inland in the northern part of the country is a plateau region. Farther east are rolling hills and plains, drained by Sava and Drava rivers, that contain Croatia's best farmland. More than a third of the country is covered by forests. Aside from timber, Croatia's natural resources include iron, bauxite, coal, and oil. Major crops include wheat, corn, sugar beets, wine grapes, and a wide variety of other crops. Croatia is a world leader in shipbuilding; other important local industries produce steel, cement, textiles, chemicals, and food products. Croatia's coastal regions have a Mediterranean climate, while inland a continental climate prevails.

In 1991, ethnic Croats made up 78 percent of Croatia's 4.8 million people. Serbs accounted for about 12 percent and Muslims a bit more than 1 percent of the population. However, since 1991 about 500,000 of Croatia's 600,000 Serbs have fled or been driven from Croatia, and they currently account for only about 2 percent of the population. Zagreb, Croatia's capital and largest city, stands on the banks of the Sava.

Independent Croatia had a violent birth. In May 1991, the country held a referendum, boycotted by local Serbs, in which more than 90 percent of those voting supported independence. An official declaration of independence came in June. By then Croatia's 600,000 Serbs were literally up in arms. They were determined to secede from Croatia and join Serbia, a goal promoted by the Serbian government in Belgrade. The Serbian army, actually the old Yugoslav National Army (JNA) from which most non-Serbs had already deserted, intervened in the fighting. This left Croatia fighting both a civil war with local Serbs and a war with neighboring Serbia. By September the

Serbs controlled three areas where they were the majority: Eastern Slavonia, near the Serbian border; part of Western Slavonia, a small pocket in the center of the country; and Krajina, between the Bosnian border and the Adriatic Sea. They immediately expelled nearly all the Croat inhabitants from those regions. In January 1992, when the UN finally arranged a cease-fire (more than a dozen already had broken down) Serb forces held about a third of Croatia. An estimated 10,000 people were dead, and more than 400,000 were homeless refugees. Many factories, roads, and other vital economic assets were destroyed. So was the tourist industry, Croatia's largest source of foreign earnings. The long, though unsuccessful, Serbian siege of Dubrovnik left many of its historic stone buildings damaged. The successful Serb siege of the city of Vukovar in Eastern Slavonia left that regional capital in ruins and forced 80,000 Croats to flee their homes.

Still, Croatia was an independent country recognized by the international community. In March 1992 a UN peacekeeping force of 14,000 began arriving in Croatia, and the JNA began its withdrawal from the country. However, the end of full-scale war and the UN presence in Croatia did not mean peace. Fighting between Serbs and Croats continued inside Croatia, while President Franjo Tudjman sent Croatian forces to join the fighting in Bosnia. It lasted both in Croatia proper and in Bosnia until 1995.

Between May and August of 1995, Croatian forces overran two of the three Serb-held enclaves inside Croatia. Now the Serbs, like the Croats several years earlier, became victims of ethnic cleansing, as the Croatian government drove about 300,000 of them from the country. In elections held in August, the Tudjman-led Croatian Democratic Union (CDU) kept its control of parliament. It was, however, a flawed campaign; critics accused the government of flagrant media bias and limiting the opposition's access to television.

Perhaps most disturbing, independent Croatia celebrated the memory of the fascist World War II Ustashe regime. Franjo

Tudjman, who as young man had fought with Tito's Communist Partisans against the Ustashe, since the 1970s had become a militant nationalist and in the 1990s embraced what he had once opposed. He called his opposition to fascism a "youthful mistake." The closest political ally of the CDU was Croatia's Party of Rights, whose members at rallies openly raised their hands in the notorious stiff-armed Nazi salute as they shouted the Nazi greetings *Sieg* and *Heil*. The Tudjman government honored the Ustashe as the forerunners of the modern Croatian state. Croatia's new flag and the uniforms of its police both recalled the Ustashe era. Former Ustashe soldiers were invited to state celebrations. Tudjman, who openly expressed hatred for both Serbs and Jews, even appointed a former high-ranking Ustashe official to parliament. Many Croats, including those who had fought with the Partisans against the Ustashe, opposed what was happening, but were afraid to speak out. As one elderly Partisan veteran commented sadly, "Today, those who should hold their heads in shame are national heroes."[3]

One of those "heroes" clearly was Franjo Tudjman, who in June 1997 was reelected Croatia's president with 61 percent of the vote. In January 1998 Croatia completed its territorial reunification when the United Nations, in accordance with the Dayton Accords, handed Eastern Slavonia back to Zagreb's control. The national soccer team provided another highlight to 1998 when it reached the semifinals of the World Cup Tournament. These developments were signs to many Croatians that their country was emerging from the dark shadows of its past. But there were other signs that those shadows were growing longer and darker. Croatia's glorification of its fascist past appalled the world's democracies. It committed massive human-rights violations as it pressed its campaign to drive all Serbs from the country in order to create an ethnically pure society. Croatia had won its independence; however, in its unrelenting pursuit of fanatical nationalist goals it lost something just as important—the tolerance and sympathy for others that are essential to a free society.

Croatia's direction began to change in 1999. In December President Tudjman died after a three-year battle with stomach cancer. Barely three weeks later, in the first week of the new century, Croatian voters turned their backs on Tudjman's Croatian Democratic Union (HDZ) and gave a plurality to the Social Democratic Party (SDP), a group composed largely of former Communists. The SDP was led by Ivica Racan, a bearded former Communist with an interest in rock music. The main reason for the HDZ's defeat was economic hardship. Croatia's economy had declined by an average of almost 3 percent per year from 1990 through 1996. After an improvement in 1997, hard times returned. Companies could not pay their bills, 20 percent of all workers were underemployed, banks were insolvent, and Croatia itself was $10 billion in debt. Meanwhile, Tudjman accumulated a vast fortune, and many of his political associates became rich as well.

Yet if economics was the main reason for his party's victory, Racan declared that he planned to change more economic policy. Aside from announcing plans to promote more social equality and fight corruption, Racan pledged to promote genuine democracy in Croatia. Specific proposals included making the justice system fairer and allowing those with differing opinions more access to the state-controlled television system. Racan also promised more cooperation with efforts to build unity in Bosnia and with the international tribunal prosecuting war crimes committed there between 1992 and 1995.

Croatia's new government was a coalition of six parties. In February 2000, the leader of one of the smaller parties, Stipe Mesic, was elected the country's president. Mesic had been imprisoned for a year under Tito. Although he served in the Tudjman regime for several years, he later became one of Tudjman's most vocal critics. With his election, Croatia had in place a regime committed to change. It also had a long list of economic and political problems serious and urgent enough to test the most resolute and skillful leaders.

Federal Republic of Yugoslavia

The Federal Republic of Yugoslavia (FRY) consists of Serbia and Montenegro, the two parts of the former Yugoslavia that had a majority Serb population. It was officially established in April 1992 and is the largest of the former Yugoslavia successor states. The FRY has a area of 39,339 square miles (102,173 square kilometers), about the size of Virginia, and a population of 10.4 million people, which means that in both area and population the FRY accounts for about 40 percent of the former Yugoslavia. Serbia, with an area of 34,116 square miles (88,361 square kilometers), about the size of Kentucky, and population of about 9.8 million people, is by far the larger of the FRY's two republics. Connecticut-sized Montenegro has an area of just 5,333 square miles (13,812 square kilometers) and a population of about 615,000.

Most of the FRY is mountainous. Its central and southern mountains are part of the Balkan range, while the coastal mountains are a branch of the Alps. The fertile Pannonian Plain covers much of the north. It is drained by the Danube and two of its major tributaries, the Sava and the Tisza. Belgrade, the FRY's capital and largest city, stands where the Sava meets the Danube. Most of the FRY has a continental climate, with cold winters and hot summers. There is heavy winter snowfall in the inland regions. The country's natural resources include oil, natural gas, coal, lead, and various metals. The major crops are corn, sugar beets, wheat, potatoes, grapes, plums, and soybeans. Farmers also raise cattle, sheep, and pigs. The FRY's main industries produce a variety of metals, machinery (including military equipment), and appliances.

Ethnic Serbs make up about 63 percent of the population, and Montenegrins another 6 percent. About 14 percent of the population is Albanian, including 90 percent of Kosovo province. Tension between Serbs and independence-minded Albanians in Kosovo became one of the FRY's most urgent problems after 1991. Hungarians, who made up a quarter of the population in the Vojvodina region along the Hungarian border, are about 4 percent of the country's total population. Two thirds of Serbia's people are Eastern Orthodox, 19 percent are Muslims, 4 percent are Catholic, and 1 percent are Protestant.

The Federal Republic of Yugoslavia has a national parliament and president and parallel governments for its constituent republics, Serbia and Montenegro. What is important to understand, however, is that since the founding of the FRY real power has rested with the Serbian government. Thus Slobodan Milosevic, the Serbian president until 1998, was and still is the real leader of the FRY. His power base is Serbia, and much of that power has depended on the control his Serbian Socialist Party (SPS) has over the Serbian parliament. For that reason, the focus of the following discussion will refer to Serbia and Milosevic's activities as Serbia's president.

It is highly debatable whether Yugoslavia, given its deep ethnic rifts, could have survived the changes that swept the Communist world in the 1980s. At the same time, there is little doubt that the hard-line ethnic policies of the Serbian government after Milosevic came to power in 1987 helped make the final split unavoidable. Once secession began in 1991, Milosevic's goal of a "Greater Serbia" involved his country in two wars, one in Croatia that lasted until 1992 and one in Bosnia that lasted until 1995. The wars cost Serbia dearly. It suffered many casualties and was flooded by refugees from the war zones. Serbia's support of ethnic cleansing turned it into an international pariah. In 1992 the FRY was denied admission to the UN. Between 1992 and 1995 Serbia was subject to UN economic sanctions that badly hurt its economy. Montenegro, Serbia's partner, suffered as well.

Serbian political life during and after the wars in Croatia and Bosnia was marked by power struggles, corruption, and repeated elections that brought little real change. Some Serbian political groups were committed to real reforms and genuine democracy, but they were unable to compete successfully in an arena dominated by ruthless former Communists and extreme nationalists. One of Milosevic's most effective weapons was the Serbian state television and radio network, which fed the people a steady diet of progovernment programs and distorted news. Elections were frequent, but not necessarily fair. Charges of electoral fraud by opposition parties in the presidential and parliamentary elections of December 1992 were to no avail. Milosevic was reelected with 57 percent of the vote, defeating a moderate candidate who had denounced ethnic cleansing, and the SPS won the largest number of seats in parliament. Nor were some of Milosevic's rivals necessarily less militant in their nationalism than he was. For example, the second-place finisher in the 1992 elections was the Serbian Radical Party (SRP) led by Vojislav Seselj. The Radical Party was so extreme that in 1993 it accused Milosevic of betraying Serbia when he finally took steps to end the Bosnian war. Another popular Milosevic opponent was Vuk Draskovic, whose Serbian Renewal Movement (SRM) supported efforts to end the Bosnian war. He and his supporters organized an antiwar rally of 20,000 people in Belgrade as early as May 1992. Yet the Renewal Movement advocated a "Greater Serbia" that would include both Croatian and Bosnian territory, although that objective supposedly would be achieved only by peaceful means. In any event, the methods Milosevic used against Draskovic were not always peaceful. In 1993 Draskovic and his wife were arrested at an antigovernment demonstration. They probably were tortured by the police before international protests forced their release.

Along with dominating and corrupting Serbian politics, Milosevic added to his country's economic hardship. In effect, he allowed his cronies to loot the country. The international economic sanctions against Serbia, which caused such hardship for ordinary Serbians, became a means for well-connected Serbs to get rich. The vehicle was government-approved smuggling. It made millions for government ministers and others close to Milosevic whose influence enabled them to bring desperately needed goods into the country and sell them at enormous profit. The well-connected also controlled state-owned enterprises and used them to get rich. Nor did these conditions change after the wars in Croatia and Bosnia ended. As one young and discouraged economist put it in mid-1997:

> Only connections count. Under the Milosevic regime, it won't do you any good to be educated and creative and inventive. You have to have connections.[4]

The results of Milosevic's economic corruption and mismanagement were disastrous. By 1997, industrial production was, at best, 40 percent of the 1989 figure, and probably much lower. Exports were a third of the prewar level. Wages also had plunged to one third of their prewar level, and many workers were not being paid at all. Unemployment stood at 40 percent. None of this affected Serbia's well-connected newly rich, who enjoyed their ill-gotten wealth in fancy Belgrade nightclubs or villas in exclusive resorts in Western Europe. What this all meant for ordinary Serbs was summed up by a forty-eight-year-old woman whose once-prosperous family was reduced to selling cigarettes in a Belgrade flea market. She told a Western reporter simply: "I sleep in tears and wake up in tears."[5]

The discontent finally was translated into opposition electoral victories in city and town elections that took place in November and December 1996. A coalition of political parties led by Vuk Draskovic, called *Zajedno* (Together), won control of fourteen major Serbian town councils, including Belgrade's. The Milosevic regime disallowed the results, but ran into a wave of opposition when it did. The resulting crisis lasted until February, when the election results were reinstated. The Belgrade town council then promptly elected Zoran Djindjic, a Draskovic ally, as mayor—the city's first non-Communist mayor since World War II.

But the opposition was unable to stick together. This gave Milosevic room to maneuver. Serbia was to have presidential elections in the fall of 1997, and Milosevic was barred by the constitution from seeking a third term. In July he therefore engineered his election by the FRY parliament as president of the Yugoslav federation. While that job previously was a figure-head post, it did not stay that way with Milosevic in office. This occurred in part because by the time of the Serbian presiden-tial elections Draskovic and Djindjic had become rivals. Their differences enabled Milosevic to manipulate the Belgrade city council and oust Djindjic from the mayoralty. In an electoral process laced with irregularities and fraud, Milosevic also engi-neered the victory of Milan Milutinovic, a trusted aide, as Ser-bian president. These developments left Milosevic still firmly in the saddle in Serbia.

To be sure, Milosevic had plenty of problems. By mid-1998 he faced real problems with Montenegro, where thirty-five-year-old Milo Djukanovic, a staunch opponent, was elected president in October 1997. Some Montenegrins even began talking about breaking with Serbia and leaving the FRY. Even more urgent, by mid-1998 Milosevic and Serbia faced an open rebellion by ethnic Albanians in Kosovo. The rebels already held control of part of the countryside and seemed capable of waging a long and costly guerrilla war. A major Ser-bian offensive in the summer of 1998 drove the rebels from their main stronghold and badly weakened them, but did not end the rebellion.

Instead, the situation in Kosovo quickly degenerated into violent chaos. The main Albanian force fighting the Serbs was the Kosovo Liberation Army (KLA). The KLA had few scruples in waging its struggle against the Serbs. It financed its opera-tions in part by being an international smuggler of heroin and waged a campaign of terror against Kosovo's minority Serb population. Part of the KLA strategy was to provoke the Ser-bians, and it succeeded. The Milosevic regime, with far greater resources, responded with a wave of terror against the Albanian population that dwarfed the KLA's violence. Serbian forces drove thousands of Albanians from their homes as part of a pol-icy of "ethnic cleansing." International pressure built against

As the Serbs swept into their towns and villages,
Albanians quickly piled into their farm vehicles and
fled across the border to escape the fighting.

the Serbs during late 1998 and early 1999. Finally, after negotiations failed to end the violence, the NATO alliance intervened. In March 1999 it began a bombing campaign against Serbia. Instead of giving in as NATO's leaders expected, the Serbs stepped up their terror and ethnic cleansing. They drove about 800,000 Albanians into neighboring countries.

NATO aircraft pounded Serbia for seventy-eight days before Milosevic finally relented in June. A NATO force of about 33,000 troops—it reached 50,000 by the end of 1999— moved into Kosovo. Its job was to restore order, enable the Albanian refugees to return home, and protect both the Albanian majority and the Serbian minority so they could find a way to live together. The NATO occupation force achieved only a part of its mission. Most Albanian refugees did return to Kosovo, but NATO troops often failed to prevent Albanians from taking revenge on the Serbs. By the end of 1999 about two thirds of the Serb population of 200,000 had fled Kosovo. They were joined in their flight by thousands of Gypsies, whom the Albanians accused of collaborating with the Serbs, and other minority groups such as ethnic Croats and non-Albanian Muslims.

As the year 2000 began, Kosovo was a grim land still torn by ethnic hatred and occupied by a foreign army able to prevent mass violence but unable to restore real peace. Meanwhile, in Belgrade, Milosevic's grip on his country began to slip. In the summer of 2000, he advanced the date of the Yugoslav presidential elections by nine months in order to take advantage of his disorganized opponents and further entrench himself in power. The tactic backfired. To almost everyone's surprise, a loose coalition of eighteen political parties united behind a single candidate, a 56-year-old scholar named Vojislav Kostunica. Kostunica's reputation for honesty and integrity, coupled with his unflinching courage in the face of violence by Milosevic supporters, gave him a wide appeal among war-weary and exhausted Serbs. In September, he stunned Milosevic by decisively winning the election. Kostunica's inauguration as Yugoslavia's president in October finally gave the people of Serbia and Montenegro hope that at last they might be able to look forward to better times.

Maps and Flags of the

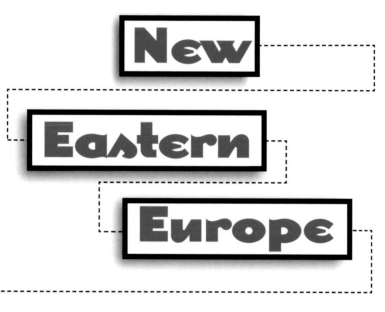

New

Eastern

Europe

Map #1 Political map of the
New Eastern Europe

Map #2 Geographical map of
the New Eastern Europe

Flags of the countries in the
New Eastern Europe

BALTIC
SEA

NORTH SEA

BALTIC HTS.

N O R T H E R N   E U R O P E A N

Oder R.

SILESIAN PLATE

Elbe R.

ORE MTNS.

SUDETEN MTNS.

Rhine R.

BOHEMIAN
PLATEAU

BOHEMIAN FOREST

Morava R.

Seine R.

Danube R.

DAN
B

ALPS

Dra

KRAS

Sava R.

Rhone R.

Po R.

DINARI

ADRIATIC SEA

APENNINES

TYRRHENIAN
SEA

**CENTRAL
AND EASTERN
EUROPE**

MEDITERRANEAN SEA

Poland

The coat of arms of Poland—a red shield with a white eagle—came into use in the middle of the thirteenth century. Almost every Polish flag in the intervening centuries has used this shield and/or its colors. The current national flag was adopted in 1919 as Poland regained its independence.

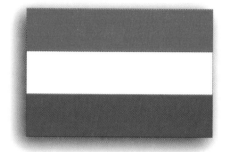

Hungary

The two historical coats of arms of Hungary provided the national colors—red, white, and green. Its tricolored flag dated from the beginning of the nineteenth century and became prominent when Hungarian independence was proclaimed in 1848 and again in 1918. The present flag dates from 1957.

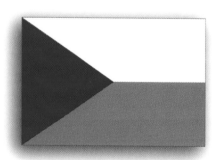

Czech Republic

Bohemians, Slovaks, and Ruthenians formed a new Slavic nation, Czechoslovakia, in 1918. Its flag, of white and red stripes, derived from the traditional Bohemian shield—red with a white lion. In 1920 a triangle was added in blue, a Slovak and Ruthenian color. The flag was reestablished in 1945.

Slovakia

In their 1948 revolution, Slovaks adopted the pan-Slavic colors of the Russian flag (white, blue, red). They also created a coat of arms in the same colors, incorporating a cross over mountains. Just before independence in 1993 Slovakia added the shield to its tricolor, to distinguish it from the Russian flag.

Slovenia

The Slovenes chose the colors of Russia as their own, but when independence was achieved in 1992 a distinctive shield was added. It contains the famous Triglav peak and waves for its coastal area. The three stars are from the coat of arms of the ancient county of Celje.

Croatia

The traditional pan-Slavic red-white-blue colors from 1848 form the background for the unique Croatian coat of arms. Adopted when Croatia became independent in 1992, the distinctive crown contains the arms of old Croatia, Dubrovnik (Ragusa), Dalmatia, Istria, and Slavonia. The checkerboard below is centuries old.

Macedonia

The national anthem refers to the rising sun of independence featured on the flag. The red and gold date from the Middle Ages, when Macedonia's shield displayed a golden lion on a red background. The flag was adopted in 1995, replacing a design that neighboring Greece believed was too similar to a sunburst design used as a Greek symbol.

Albania

The double-headed eagle has been a symbol of power for centuries. Albania inherited it from the Byzantine Empire, of which it was once part. The fifteenth-century Albanian hero Skanderbeg (George Kastrioti) resisted Turkish invasions for years under this flag. It was reestablished in 1912 and most recently readopted in 1992.

Bulgaria

National independence was achieved in 1878 with the assistance of Russia. In gratitude, the Bulgarians chose the Russian tricolor as their own, substituting green for the blue stripe. White is for peace and freedom, red for struggle and courage, and green for agriculture. The current flag dates from 1990.

Romania

In the revolution of 1848 a blue-yellow-red tricolor was briefly adopted by Romania, based on traditional heraldic colors of Walachia and Moldova. In 1867 the tricolor was again recognized. It has continued as the national flag ever since, although frequently displaying the coat of arms of royal or Communist regimes.

Yugoslavia

The "Land of the Southern Slavs" was created in 1918 under the horizontal tricolor of the traditional Slavic blue-white-red. Different emblems appeared in the center of the flag until 1992, when the current constitution was adopted. Serbia and Montenegro, the constituent republics of Yugoslavia, have flags of their own.

A multiethnic land that had not been independent for centuries, Bosnia proclaimed statehood in 1992. After years of civil war, its original flag was replaced in 1995. The new design has the European colors (yellow and dark blue) and a triangle that recalls the shape of the country.

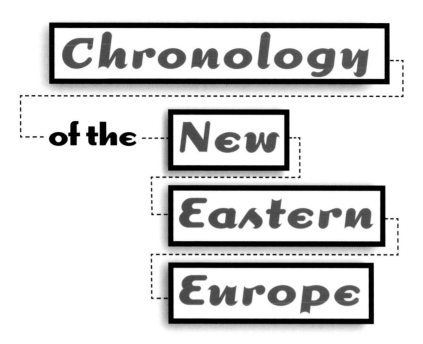

1989

Poland

- Communist government legalizes Solidarity and agrees to free parliamentary elections.
- Solidarity wins elections overwhelmingly.
- Majority non-Communist government takes office.
- Economic reform, including "shock therapy," begins.

Hungary

- Communist government removes barbed wire along Hungary's border with Austria.
- Communist Party dissolves itself, in effect ending its rule.

Czechoslovakia

- Communist regime collapses in late November and early December.
- Vaclav Havel elected president by parliament.

Bulgaria
- Hard-line Communist leaders removed from office by reformers who promise free elections.

Romania
- Dictator Nicolae Ceaușescu overthrown and executed.

East Germany
- Communist regime opens the Berlin Wall on November 9 after removing hard-line leader Erich Honecker from office. The entire party leadership resigns a month later.

Yugoslavia
- President Milosevic limits the autonomy of Kosovo province.

1990

Poland
- Local elections are held.
- Wojciech Jaruzelski resigns as president.
- Lech Walesa elected president.

Hungary
- Parliamentary elections won by pro–free-market parties.

Czechoslovakia
- President Vaclav Havel delivers dramatic first "New Year's Address."
- Parliamentary elections won by Civic Forum (Czech)/Public Against Violence (Slovak) alliance.
- Parliament reelects Havel president.

Romania
- Parliamentary elections, marred by fraud and intimidation, won by the National Salvation Front led by Ion Iliescu.

- Antigovernment protests met by government-organized violence that leaves several people dead.

Bulgaria
- Parliamentary elections won by Bulgaria's Socialist Party (the reorganized Communists).
- Parliament elects Zhelya Zhelev president.

Yugoslavia
- Milosevic reelected president of Serbia; Franjo Tudjman elected president of Croatia.

Macedonia
- A coalition of nationalist parties wins the parliamentary elections and begins moving Macedonia toward secession from Yugoslavia.

Bosnia-Herzegovena
- Alija Izetbegovic elected president.

1991

Poland
- Solidarity calls a general strike to protest the hardships caused by "shock therapy."
- Parliamentary elections are held, but voter turnout is low.

Czechoslovakia
- Last Soviet/Russian troops leave the country.

Bulgaria
- Adopts new constitution.

Albania
- Despite still being under Communist rule, holds multi-party parliamentary elections. Communists win but the

non-Communist Democratic Party of Albania finishes a strong second.

Yugoslavia
- Slovenia and Croatia declare their independence from Yugoslavia.
- Fighting breaks out between the Yugoslav army and Croatian and Slovenian forces.
- Macedonia and Bosnia declare independence.
- Yugoslavia ceases to exist. In its place are five independent states, including one called the Federal Republic of Yugoslavia, consisting of Serbia and Montenegro.

Slovenia
- Adopts new constitution.

Macedonia
- Adopts new constitution.
- Parliament elects Kiro Gligorov president.

1992

Poland
- Free-market reforms lead to more strikes.
- "Little Constitution," a temporary document intended to bridge the gap until a new constitution can be worked out, is adopted.

Hungary
- Parliament passes a law providing compensation for people whose property was seized between 1939 and 1989.

Czechoslovakia
- Parliamentary elections reveal growing Slovak nationalist sentiments.

- Vladimir Meciar becomes prime minister of the Slovak half of the country. Vaclav Klaus becomes the prime minister of the Czech half.
- Parliament does not reelect Vaclav Havel as president.
- Parliament passes a law dividing the country into two independent countries. Czechoslovakia ceases to exist. In its place are the Czech Republic and the Slovak Republic.

Romania
- Parliamentary elections, narrowly won by a divided National Salvation Front.

Bulgaria
- Former Communist dictator Todor Zhivkov convicted of corruption and briefly sent to prison.
- Zhelya Zhelev reelected president directly by the country's voters.
- Parliamentary elections won by the non-Communist Union of Democratic Forces led by Zhelev.

Albania
- Parliamentary elections won by the non-Communist Democratic Party of Albania.
- Parliament elects DPA leader Sali Berisha president.

Slovenia
- Parliamentary elections won by the non-Communist Liberal Democratic Party.
- Voters elect Milan Kucan president.

Bosnia-Herzegovena
- Civil war begins.
- Bosnian Croats and Serbs both declare existence of their own "republics."

Croatia

- UN arranges cease-fire that ends Croatia's war with Yugoslav (Serbian) forces and follows up by sending a peacekeeping force.

Federal Republic of Yugoslavia (Serbia and Montenegro)

- Adopts new constitution
- Denied admission to the United Nations.
- Antiwar rally by opposition groups in Belgrade.
- Serbian presidential and parliamentary elections won respectively by Slobodan Milosevic and his Serbian Socialist Party.

1993

Poland

- Parliament adopts strict anti-abortion law.
- The last Soviet/Russian combat troops leave the country.
- Left Democratic Alliance wins parliamentary elections.

Czech Republic

- Vaclav Klaus continues as prime minister.
- Parliament elects Vaclav Havel president.

Slovak Republic

- Parliament elects Michal Kovac president.
- Kovac appoints Josef Moravcik prime minister.
- Parliamentary elections won by Vladimir Meciar's Movement for a Democratic Slovakia. Meciar regains the post of prime minister.

Macedonia

- Admitted to the United Nations.
- The United States sends marines to guard the border with Serbia's province of Kosovo.

1994

Poland
- Nationwide strikes protest economic hardship.
- A Solidary demonstration in Warsaw ends in violence.

Hungary
- Parliamentary elections won by the Hungarian Socialist Party.

Bulgaria
- Parliamentary elections won by the Bulgarian Socialist Party.

Macedonia
- Greece begins economic blockade.
- Holds parliamentary and presidential elections. Kiro Gligorov reelected president; Alliance for Macedonia wins a majority in parliament.

1995

Poland
- Alexander Kwasniewski is elected president, defeating Walesa.

Slovak Republic
- One of President Michal Kovac's sons is kidnapped in a plot almost certainly hatched by Prime Minister Vladimir Meciar.

Macedonia
- Greece ends economic blockade.
- President Kiro Gligorov seriously injured in an assassination attempt.

Bosnia-Herzegovena
- Serbs massacre thousands of Muslims in the city of Srebrenica.
- Dayton Accords finally end the civil war.

Croatia
- Croatian forces overrun two of three Serb-held enclaves; ethnic cleansing of Serbs follows.
- The Croatian Democratic Union led by Franjo Tudjman wins parliamentary elections amid accusations of harassment by opposition parties.

1996

Poland
- Socialist-controlled parliament changes the law, making it easier to get an abortion.

Czech Republic
- In Parliamentary elections, Civic Democratic Party under Vaclav Klaus does poorly but still wins a plurality.
- Vaclav Havel has lung surgery.

Romania
- Emil Constantinescu is elected president, defeating Ion Iliescu. Constantinescu's Democratic Convention wins the parliamentary elections.

Bulgaria
- Petar Stoyanov elected president.

Slovenia
- Parliamentary elections again won by the Liberal Democratic Party.

Federal Republic of Yugoslavia
- Opposition parties win elections in fourteen Serbian cities and towns, including Belgrade.

1997

Poland
- Gdansk shipyard is closed due to bankruptcy.
- New constitution adopted.
- Invited to join NATO.
- Solidarity coalition wins parliamentary elections.
- Parliament restores the restrictive abortion law of 1993.

Hungary
- Invited to join NATO.
- Voters, in referendum, overwhelmingly support joining NATO.

Czech Republic
- Vaclav Havel reelected president by parliament.
- Invited to join NATO

Bulgaria
- Parliamentary elections won by the Union of Democratic Forces.

Albania
- Several investment schemes collapse, causing economic turmoil.
- Parliament reelects Sali Berisha to a second term as president.
- Antigovernment protesters seize control of much of the southern part of the country. It takes the intervention of the Organization for Security and Cooperation in Europe to restore order.

- Parliamentary elections won by the Socialist Party. Berisha resigns as president.
- Parliament elects Rexhep Mejdani president.

Slovenia
- President Milan Kucan reelected.

Croatia
- President Franjo Tudjman is overwhelmingly reelected.

Federal Republic of Yugoslavia
- Belgrade town council elects opposition politician Zoran Djindjic mayor.
- Slobodan Milosevic engineers his election as federal president.
- Milosevic gets the Belgrade city council to dismiss Djindjic from his post as mayor.
- Milan Milutinovic, a Milosevic aide, is elected president of Serbia in elections marred by irregularities.
- Milo Djukanovic, a Milosevic foe, is elected president of Montenegro.

1998

Hungary
- Hungarian Civic Party (Fidesz), led by Viktor Orban, wins parliamentary elections.

Czech Republic
- Parliamentary elections, narrowly won by Social Democrats (the reorganized former Communists). Party leader Milos Zeman becomes prime minister.

Slovak Republic
- President Michal Kovac's term ends, but a bitterly divided parliament is unable to choose a successor.

- Parliamentary elections result in Vladimir Meciar and the MDS losing power to Mikulas Dzurinda and the Slovak Democratic Union.

Romania
- Continued economic problems lead to a change in prime ministers.

Croatia
- Croatia takes control of Eastern Slavonia, completing its territorial unification.

Federal Republic of Yugoslavia
- Ethnic Albanians in Kosovo begin armed struggle for independence, tying down 50,000 Serbian troops.

Albania
- Voters approve a new constitution.

Macedonia
- Parliamentary elections won by the Internal Macedonian Revolutionary Organization, led by Ljubco Grigorievski.

1999

Poland
- Officially joins NATO.

Hungary
- Officially joins NATO.

Czech Republic
- Officially joins NATO.

Slovak Republic
- Rudolf Schuster elected president, defeating Vladimir Meciar.

Romania
- Environmental disasters in January and March when poisons spill into the country's rivers.

Albania
- Half a million refugees from Kosovo pour into the country during the NATO bombing campaign against Serbia.

Macedonia
- Boris Trajkovski elected president.

Croatia
- Franjo Tudjman dies.

Federal Republic of Yugoslavia
- Serb forces driven from Kosovo as a result of the NATO bombing campaign lasting for 78 days (from late March to June).

2000

Croatia
- Parliamentary elections won by the opposition Social Democratic Union. Ivaca Racan becomes prime minister.
- Stipe Mesic elected president.

Federal Republic of Yugoslavia
- Vojislav Kostunica defeats Slobodan Milosevic and becomes president.

Poland
- Aleksander Kwasniewski reelected president.

A

Alia, Ramiz (1925–)

President of Albania, 1985–1992. Alia was born into a poor Muslim family and joined Albania's Communist guerrilla movement in 1944. After the Communist takeover he established himself as an outstanding member of the party's younger generation of leaders. He rose through the ranks, avoided becoming one of the many victims of Enver Hoxha's paranoid outbursts, and emerged as the dictator's successor when Hoxha died in 1985. If Alia's main achievement prior to 1985 was surviving in Albania's dangerous political waters, his greatest accomplishment while in power was being flexible enough to help Albania to avoid violence as its Communist dictatorship crumbled in the late 1980s and early 1990s. The new regime later charged Alia with genocide and crimes against humanity. With more than a thousand other prisoners, he escaped from detention during the turmoil that swept Albania in March 1997 and fled to Sweden. The charges against him were dropped by Albania's new socialist government in October of that year.

Aralica, Ivan (1930–)

One of Croatia's leading modern novelists. Aralica's work often focuses on Croatia's peasantry. He uses a variety of historical settings to discuss present-day moral and ethical conflicts.

Belgrade

Capital and largest city (population 1.16 million) of the Federal Republic of Yugoslavia and Serbia. Belgrade traces its roots back two thousand years to fortresses built by the Celts, Illyrians, and Romans. It is strategically located where the Danube and Sava rivers meet. Conquerors have left many scars on Belgrade; it has been destroyed and rebuilt about forty times in its troubled history. Belgrade did not become Serbia's capital until 1403, after the disastrous Battle of Kosovo Polje. The Turks took the city in 1521 and made it their chief strategic fortress in the Balkans. Repeated efforts to liberate the city in the eighteenth century brought only temporary successes, and the Turks fought to hold the city against both Austrians and Serbs with bitter determination. Not until 1815 did the Turks leave, and even then they garrisoned a fortress in the city until 1867. Belgrade became Serbia's capital again in 1882 and the capital of Yugoslavia after World War I. It remains Serbia's cultural, political, industrial, and commercial center and is known for its churches, parks, palaces, and museums. Despite Serbia's many troubles, it is a lively city, at least for Serbia's newly rich who have profited during the Milosevic era.

Berisha, Sali (1944–)

President of Albania, 1992–1997. Berisha was an internationally recognized cardiologist before entering politics. As part of Communist Albania's privileged elite, he was one of a select few allowed to travel outside the country. Berisha founded Albania's Democratic Party in 1990. As a politician he was known for dramatic speeches delivered in a booming baritone voice and for his rugged good looks. As Albania's president he focused on introducing free-market reforms. "Salu," as he usually was called, also was known for his short temper. In office Berisha became increasingly inflexible and dictatorial, which helped provoke the turmoil that led to his party's electoral defeat and his resignation from office in 1997.

Bialowieza Forest and National Park

Thousands of years ago a huge forest stretched from Europe's Atlantic coast to the Ural Mountains. A great variety of plant and animal life thrived under a towering canopy formed by oak, ash, and elm trees. The forest is almost all gone today; the main exception is the Bialowieza Forest that straddles the border between Poland and Belarus. Forty percent of the forest's 580 square miles (1,500 square kilometers) is in Poland. Part of the Polish forest is the Bialowieza National Park, where no hunting or felling of trees is allowed. Inside the park is a smaller nature reserve of about 35 square miles (90 square kilometers), where no visitors are allowed without a park guide. Outside the park hunting of deer and some other animals is permitted.

There is some irony in the fact that the pristine Bialowieza Forest still stands in two of Europe's most polluted countries. It survived mainly because Polish kings and Russian tsars, and later Polish and Soviet commissars, protected it as their private hunting ground. Today deer, moose, wild horses, boar, and bison (Europe's largest animal) still graze and forage in the for-

*Forestry students are allowed into
Bialowicza to study this primeval forest.*

est's grassy areas and swamps. The people of Poland, even as they busily go about adjusting to the enormous changes in their country since 1989, have taken the time to pay attention to this national treasure. Recently a mass campaign to extend the national park to all of Poland's share of the forest was a partial success: The size of the park was doubled.

Birthrates

While many regions of the world suffer from overpopulation and exploding birthrate, Eastern Europe began its post-Communist era with the opposite problem: a birthrate that was far too low. In 1995, ten of the region's twelve countries had a birthrate below the replacement level (2.1 births per woman). Only Albania and Macedonia (exactly at 2.1 births per woman) were exceptions. This would not be a problem, and would in fact be welcome, if Eastern Europe was overpopulated, but that is not the case. The causes of this problem are complex, but probably have more to do with modern urbanized living than any other single factor.

That may explain why a collapsing birthrate is one problem Eastern Europe shares with the three largest European countries of the former Soviet Union (Russia, Ukraine, and Belarus) and with many prosperous countries of Western Europe (Germany, Britain, France, and Italy, to name a few).

Blandiana, Ana (1942–)

Romanian poet. During the Communist era, Blandiana was widely admired both for the quality of her poetry and her courage in standing up to government pressure on artists. After the fall of Nicolae Ceauşescu in 1989, she actively opposed the dictatorial measures of the Iliescu government. One collection of her poetry, *The Hour of Sand: Selected Poems, 1969–1989*, is available in English.

Bochev, Dimitur (1944–)

Bulgarian novelist and essayist. After years as an active dissident, and many prison terms, Bochev emigrated to the West in 1972. He continued his anti-Communist activity abroad by broadcasting for Radio Free Europe and contributing, with other Eastern European exiles, to the famous anti-Communist journal *Continent*. A major theme in his work is how an exile feels alienated from two worlds, the one he left behind and the foreign world where he is trying to build a new life.

Boban, Matte (1940–1997)

Leader of Croatians in Bosnia. Although less well known than either Radovan Karadzic or Alija Izetbegovic, Boban was to Bosnia's Croatians what Karadzic was to its Serbs and Izetbegovic was to its Muslims. A former salesman, Boban was handpicked by Franjo Trudjman in 1992 to form a separate Croatian enclave in Bosnia. Called the Croatian Community of Herzeg-Bosna, the enclave briefly claimed to be an independent nation and had its own flag and army. In reality, Boban successfully worked to integrate the enclave into Croatia. Muslims and Serbs were ousted from the government and police, Croatian was declared the official language, and the Croatian kuna the enclave's currency. In 1993, Boban's troops attacked Bosnian Muslim forces that supposedly were their allies in order to expand the territory under Croatian control. The fighting largely destroyed the city of Mostar, which according to the Dayton Accords, is the capital of the current Muslim-Croat Federation. Boban was implicated in the murder of Muslim civilians and removed from office after intense American pressure.

Bratislava

Capital and largest city (population 452,000) of the Slovak Republic. Bratislava stands on the banks of the Danube near the juncture of the Slovak Republic, Austria, and Hungary. Vienna is about 40 miles (64 kilometers) upstream. Oddly, although today it is the capital of a Slovak state, for most of its history Bratislava was not a Slovak city. Almost two thousand years ago the Romans had a settlement where Bratislava stands. In the ninth century it was a stronghold of the Slavic Great Moravian Empire. Thereafter, for more than a thousand years, it was under Hungarian control. After the Ottoman conquest of Buda (one of the two cities that in the nineteenth century became Budapest) in 1541, Bratislava was the Hungarian capital until 1784. Notwithstanding its large role in Hungarian history, until the nineteenth century Bratislava was a largely German city. In fact, the city had the German name of Pressburg until the end of World War I. In 1918, when Bratislava became part of Czechoslovakia, about half its population was Slovak. It did not become a majority Slovak city until after World War II.

Bratislava has long been a trading center and since the nineteenth century an industrial center as well. The Czechoslovak Communist regime turned it into a major armaments manufacturer. Unlike Prague, the Czech capital, Bratislava bears many scars of dreary Communist-style planning and building.

Bucharest

Capital and largest city (population 2 million) of Romania. Notwithstanding tales that it was founded by an ancient shepherd name "Bucar" (the Romanian word *bucurie* means "joy"),

*Ceauşescu's massive unfinished Palace of the People
in the middle of Bucharest*

Bucharest probably dates from the late fourteenth century. It became the capital of Walachia in the late seventeenth century and in 1861 the capital of a united, though still not fully independent, Romania. Bucharest reached its high point in the early 1900s when it underwent a surge of development. The Romanians looked to France for ideas and brought in French architects to direct much of the building. Their model was Paris. Broad tree-lined boulevards replaced narrow, winding streets and alleys, landscaped parks were laid out, and many fine stone buildings were constructed. In the years just before World War II Bucharest was known as the "Paris of the Balkans."

Bucharest's golden age was brief. The city was hit by an earthquake in 1940. Allied bombing during World War II and another earthquake in 1977 took a further toll. In the 1980s the monstrous building projects of Nicolae Ceauşescu, designed to turn the city into a model socialist capital, cost Bucharest many of its historic landmarks before they were ended by the 1989 revolution. Today Bucharest remains Romania's main industrial and communications center.

Budapest

Capital and largest city (population 2 million) of Hungary. Budapest straddles the Danube just south of the majestic Danube Bend. The modern city was formed in 1873 when Buda on the west bank and Pest on the east bank were merged into a single municipality. Buda traditionally was a residential area where government buildings and the palaces of Hungary's nobility stood. Pest was a commercial and industrial area. Buda became Hungary's capital in 1361. It reached a zenith as a cultural center in the fifteenth century under Matthias Corvinus. Budapest dates from Roman times and has seen more than its share of hardship. The Mongols destroyed it in 1241. The Turks, who conquered Pest in 1526 and Buda in 1541, left the city in ruins when they yielded it to the Hapsburg armies in 1686. About 70 percent of Buda, including historic palaces and churches, was damaged or destroyed during World War II, as were all eight of the bridges spanning the Danube. The city also was the main theater of the Hungarian Revolution of 1956,

A view of the Hungarian parliament buildings across the Danube

when Russian tanks, which drove the Germans from the city in 1945, returned to crush Hungary's attempt to liberate itself from Communism.

Budapest has a long history as a theatrical, artistic, and musical center. It was here that Franz Liszt (1811–1886), one of Hungary's greatest composers and probably the greatest pianist of his time, wrote the *Hungarian Coronation Mass* for the coronation of Emperor Franz Joseph in 1867. The city also is known for its parks, especially Margaret Island in the middle of the Danube, where writers, artists, composers, philosophers, and even kings have come for inspiration. After forty years of suffocating Communist rule, Budapest returned to life in the 1990s. Nightclubs and restaurants have opened and cultural life has revived. At the same time, Budapest must now cope with the traffic, noise, social problems, and inflated cost of living that have arrived as the baggage of free-wheeling capitalism.

Buzek, Jerzy (1940–)

Prime Minister of Poland, 1997– . Buzek was a chemistry professor before becoming involved in politics. He first made his mark as an extremely able organizer for Solidarity and was the chairman of its first congress in Gdansk. After the 1981 crackdown on Solidarity, Buzek went underground; he was one of the few Solidarity leaders who managed to avoid arrest. He  became prime minister after the Solidarity Election Action Party won the 1997 parliamentary elections. He is a staunch advocate of free-market ideas and has promised to sell enough state companies to increase the percentage of the Polish economy in private hands. Another major challenge Buzek faces is getting along with President Marian Kwasniewski, a former Communist.

Café Slavia

The century-old Café Slavia in Prague was a gathering place for generations of Czech artists and intellectuals before closing in 1990. Its name, "Slavia," was chosen to stress a Czech identity independent of Austrian and German influences at a time when the Czech lands were part of Austria-Hungary. During the 1970s dissidents opposed to Communist rule regularly came to the café to talk and plan as they drank strong coffee enveloped in clouds of cigarette smoke. They included the writer Pavel Kohout, who set important scenes in two of his novels at the Slavia, and Vaclav Havel, the playwright and essayist who later became his country's president. After ten years of forced exile, Kohout returned to Prague in 1989 and immediately went to the café because "I was sure my friends would be there—and they were."[1] When the renovated café finally reopened in late 1997 the old-timers returned to recall the past and also look to the future with a new generation of Prague's creative set. Havel, hospitalized with pneumonia on opening night, sent greetings to the patrons. He arrived at the café to relax at a window table soon after his recovery.

Constantinescu, Emil (1939–)

President of Romania, 1996– . Constantinescu was born in Moldova. He earned a doctorate in geology and established an international reputation as a geologist. He also holds a law degree. After 1989 his anti-Communist credentials were stronger than those of most other Romanian politicians. Although he had been a party member, he never held a position in the party. In 1989 he was one of the few Romanian professors to take an open and active role in the demonstrations against President Ceauşescu. In 1990 he became the rector of the University of Bucharest. Two years later, as the leader of a coalition of anti-Communist parties, he unsuccessfully challenged Ion Iliescu for the presidency, winning about 40 percent of the vote. He turned the table in the 1996 elections, helped in part by his excellent performance against Iliescu in four television debates. In contrast to the sixty-five-year-old Iliescu, Constantinescu, nine years younger, presented a fresh image as he hammered at Iliescu on issues such as health care, poverty, and a lack of moral leadership. After his election he told the Romanian people that reforms alone were not enough: the country had to adopt a "different mentality . . . in which fundamental values would be honesty and the capacity to work."[2]

Cracow

Although only Poland's third-largest city in size, Cracow is its second city in importance. Its history goes back more than a thousand years to a settlement that developed at the junction of two trade routes: one running from western Europe to Byzantium and the other from southern Europe to the Baltic Sea. It became Poland's capital in 1038. In 1364 King Casimir the Great founded what eventually was called the Jagiellonian University, Eastern Europe's second university, in Cracow. Although Poland's capital was moved to Warsaw in 1596, its kings and queens continued to be crowned and buried in Cracow until the nineteenth century. Cracow was the only major city in Poland to escape massive destruction in World War II, and its medieval Gothic churches and other old buildings and monuments remain intact. They include the fourteenth-century Wawel Cathedral, the coronation place and tomb for Poland's royalty, and the sixteenth century Wawel Castle, which is built in the Italian Renaissance style. Both stand on a hill overlooking the Vistula. A vibrant part of Cracow's history is missing, however: the Jewish quarter, where Jews lived and contributed to Cracow's life for more than six hundred years before their community was destroyed in the Holocaust.

Cracow's city center is ringed by a graceful green area called the *Planty*, which was planted in the nineteenth century when the old medieval city walls were torn down. The main blot on the city is the pollution from the giant Sendzimir steel works, established by the Communist regime in 1949 and a grimy monument to the flaws of Soviet-style planning.

Danube River

The Danube is the second-longest river in Europe (after the Volga) and by far the most important river in Eastern Europe. Napoleon called the Danube the "king of Europe's rivers," and he had a point. The Danube, twice as long as the Rhine, is to Eastern Europe what the Mississippi is to the United States, the Volga is to Russia, and the Yangtze is to China. The only major European river that runs west to east, the Danube is 1,770 miles (2,848 kilometers) long. It rises in the Black Forest region of southwestern Germany and flows through Germany, Austria, Slovakia, Hungary, Serbia, Romania, Bulgaria, and Ukraine before reaching the Black Sea. With its more than three hun-

The Danube in Budapest, Hungary

dred tributaries it drains an area of more than 320,000 square miles (829,000 square kilometers) where more than 80 million people live.

In Roman times the Danube formed part of the Empire's border with the barbarian world. Vienna, Budapest, and Belgrade (under different names) were military camps on the river guarding the Roman frontier. In medieval times the Danube was an important trade route linking Europe to the East. The Turkish conquest of the Balkans blocked that route, and it remained blocked until the Turks were pushed back. The river then regained its importance as a trade highway. There were a number of attempts in the nineteenth and twentieth centuries to promote international cooperation on the use of the Danube.

During the Communist era the Danube was the scene of two environmentally damaging projects. The first was the enormous Gabcikovo-Nagymaros hydroelectric project begun jointly by Czechoslovakia and Hungary in the 1970s. The project called for two dams, one in each country. However, it posed serious environmental problems, including the destruction of valuable wetlands and damage to central Europe's largest aquifer. After the region's Communist regimes collapsed, Czechoslovakia, and then Slovakia, where Gabcikovo is located, finished their part of the project. Hungary stopped its construction at Nagymaros in 1989 and backed out of the project completely in 1992 for environmental and cost reasons. The dispute over the project between the two nations ended up at the International Court of Justice at The Hague. The court, in a complicated decision, said both countries had violated their original treaty. In March 1998, Hungary and Slovakia agreed to finish the Hungarian part of the project in eight years. That decision provoked a huge protest rally in Budapest. The ultimate fate of this controversial and expensive project remains uncertain.

There is no dispute about the second Danube project: the decision by Romanian dictator Ceauşescu to turn the Danube delta into farmland. The huge delta, where the Danube splits into three arms, covers an area of more than 1,660 square miles (4,300 square kilometers). It is a maze of marshes, reeds, and sandbars that forms Europe's largest wetland west of Russia's Volga River. Much of the delta's plant and animal life is unique, and it is a meeting ground for vast flocks of migratory birds. In the mid-1980s Ceauşescu decided to drain large parts of the delta in order to grow wheat and rice. The project damaged more than 240,000 acres (97,000 hectares) before it was cancelled after Ceauşescu's fall. Scientists and engineers from several countries have since joined an international effort to restore the wetlands. The project seems to be moving ahead successfully and may provide a model for the restoration of natural habitats on other major world rivers. Experts from the United States involved in restoring floodplains along the Mississippi have taken a keen interest in the Danube delta project.

Dimitrova, Blaga (1922–)

Bulgarian poet, novelist, dramatist, biographer, and translator. Dimitrova is the author of thirty volumes of poetry, as well as numerous novels, biographies (some written jointly with her husband, Yordan Vasilev), and plays. One of her major themes is the danger of replacing human values with ideology. Despite the Bulgarian Communist regime's refusal to allow many of her books to be published at home, Dimitrova achieved an international reputation and won many prizes for her work. After the fall of the Communist regime she became involved in politics and served as Bulgaria's vice president from 1992 until her resignation in 1993. She claimed she was not consulted enough while in office.

Djindjic, Zoran (1952–)

Yugoslavian politician. Born in Bosnia, Djindjic attended university in Belgrade before earning a doctorate at the University of Konstanz in Germany. His independent political positions as a student during his Belgrade days cost him a year in prison. In 1989 he was one of the founders of the Democratic Party, a group committed to a democratic political system, freedom of the press, and human rights. Although he was counted among Yugoslavia's few major opposition political leaders, Djindjic, a generally low-key person who prefers compromise to confrontation, was reluctant to criticize Milosevic and the Socialist Party. This finally changed in 1996, when Djindjic decided that the Socialists were ruining his country. His public criticism led to a four-month suspended jail sentence. In February 1997, as part of the *Zajedno* (Together) coalition led by Vuk Drasovic, Djindjic was elected mayor of Belgrade. However, Djindjic and Drasovic had a falling out, which enabled Milosevic to engineer Djindjic's dismissal in October. Since then. Drasovic's views have become increasingly marginal—he has called for the restoration of the Serbian monarchy—leaving Djindjic as Yugoslavia's leading opposition politician.

Drnovsek, Janez (1950–)

Prime Minister of Slovenia, 1992– . Drnovsek holds a doctorate in economics and has had professional experience in the banking and construction industries. In 1990 he took the lead in founding Slovenia's Liberal Democratic Party, a group that grew out of a Communist youth movement but which completely rejected its old thinking in favor of liberal and free-market ideas. Drnovsek strengthened his party in 1994 when he organized a merger with three smaller groups to form a new party called Liberal Democracy of Slovenia.

Dzurinda, Mikulas (1955–)

Prime Minister of the Slovak Republic, 1998– . Dzurinda received his higher education at Czechoslovakia's Traffic and Communications University. He held a variety of posts dealing with traffic, communications, and public works as an official in the Czechoslovakian and Slovak governments before becoming Slovak Minister of Traffic, Communications, and Public Works in 1994. He became the leader of the Slovak Democratic Union (SDK) upon its founding in 1997 and prime minister of the Slovak Republic in October 1998.

Environmental Pollution

Just as in the former Soviet Union, Communism left Eastern Europe with some of the world's worst environmental pollution. The most intense region of industrial pollution was a coal and steel producing region that begins in the former East Germany and runs through the northern parts of the Czech and Slovak Republics and into southern Poland. Poland probably exited from Communism as Europe's most polluted nation. In its Silesia region, men who worked in steel mills, power stations, and chemical plants were dying of cancer, heart disease, and emphysema in their thirties and forties. Conditions in parts of Romania were equally bad. In the notorious "black town" of Copsa Mica, antiquated factories poured out 30,000 tons of soot a year; it quickly covered anyone who spent any time out of doors and covered the ground as far as 15 miles (24 kilometers) away. The situation was about as bad in the Czech town of Ostrava near the Polish border, the victim of pollution from metallurgy factories and thirty-five coal mines. Eastern Europe was a region of rivers polluted by sewage and heavy metals, forests ruined by acid rain, coastlines polluted by sewage and industrial wastes, and cities suffocating under blankets of polluted air. The damage extended into the Black Sea, where the fishing industry was in crisis. Some conditions have improved during the 1990s, including in Poland where many polluting factories have gone bankrupt. But the cleanup job is immense, and few resources are available for it.

Esterhazy, Peter (1950–)

Hungarian novelist, short-story writer, and essayist. Esterhazy is known as an innovator and experimenter in literary style. Since the late 1980s some of his work has been translated into English.

Geremek, Bronislaw (1932–)

Foreign Minister of Poland, 1977– . Geremek is one of Poland's few remaining Jews. Many of his relatives, including his father, were murdered during the Holocaust; Geremek survived when he and his mother escaped from the Warsaw Ghetto in 1943. Geremek received a university education in Poland and continued his studies at the Sorbonne in Paris. He is a historian and expert on medieval France and speaks perfect French. He remained in Poland even after the government's 1968 anti-Semitic campaign, but quit the Communist Party at the end of the year after the Warsaw Pact invasion of Czechoslovakia. When the Solidarity movement began he was one of only a few intellectuals willing to help the union. He was jailed for a year after the 1981 crackdown on Solidarity. Geremek's many tasks as foreign minister include easing Poland into NATO without antagonizing Russia and making sure that Poland meets the European Union's requirements for admission.

German Democratic Republic (East Germany)

After World War II, the victorious Allies divided Germany into four occupation zones. In 1949 the American, British, and French zones were united into a independent Federal Republic of Germany. The Soviet Union turned their zone into a Communist-dominated satellite, thereby making it a part of Eastern Europe. Berlin, Germany's former capital, which was surrounded entirely by the Soviet zone, also was divided into four zones. The American, British, and French zones became West Berlin, while the Soviet zone became East Berlin, the capital of East Germany. In 1961, the Soviets and East Germans built the Berlin Wall to physically cut off West Berlin from East Germany and prevent East Germans from escaping to the West via Berlin. The Berlin Wall stood for twenty-eight years as the most recognized symbol of the Cold War. When the desperate East German government finally opened the wall in November 1989, Communism was collapsing everywhere in Eastern Europe. Within a year, East Germany disappeared when Germany was reunified. Since then Germany has spent hundreds of billions of dollars to rebuild eastern Germany, an amount that dwarfs the aid and investment received by the other countries of Eastern Europe. Still, the process of integration has not been easy. Despite undeniable progress, unemployment is double that of western Germany and productivity is far lower. There also have been tensions between former West and East Germans who lived as separate nations for almost two generations. German reunification in effect means that East Germany has left Eastern Europe, but some East European problems—from environmental pollution to an inability to adjust to life in a free market economy—have not left eastern Germany.

Germans

The Germans and their ancestors have roots in Europe that stretch backward deep into ancient times. Prior to A.D. 950 the Germans generally lived west of the Elbe River. In the four centuries that followed, they colonized territory to the east, moving into Bohemia, Silesia, Pomerania, Prussia, and Austria. They also established scattered communities in Hungary and the Balkans.

Often this process was peaceful; Eastern European rulers welcomed German settlers, who were skilled craftsmen, farmers, and merchants. The large number of Germans who settled in Eastern European cities and towns, especially in Poland, gave them a distinctly German character. Sometimes the process was not peaceful, such as the conquest of Prussia by the Teutonic Knights in the thirteenth century. Germans lived in Eastern Europe both in independent states where they were the rulers, such as Prussia and Austria, and as minorities in states ruled by other national groups, such as Poland and Hungary.

The Germans contributed enormously to the economic and cultural development of Eastern Europe, as they did to Europe as a whole. For centuries the relationship between them and other ethnic groups generally were no worse than ethnic relations in Eastern Europe as a whole. This changed calamitously with the rise to power in Germany of Adolf Hitler and the Nazi Party. Nazi German conquests, accompanied by persecution, mass murder and genocide, to which was added the enormous destruction from the fighting of World War II, spelled the end the German communities in Eastern Europe when the Nazis finally were defeated. Germany's borders were shifted eastward. Millions of Germans living in Prussia (divided between Poland and the Soviet Union), Pomerania, and Silesia (both turned over to Poland) were expelled westward to within Germany's shrunken borders. The Germans of Bohemia, which belonged to Czechoslovakia, met the same fate. The Germans of the German Democratic Republic (East Germany) were fated to live under Communism and Soviet control for over forty years.

Since the collapse of Communism and Germany's reunification, Germany's influence in Eastern Europe has grown, primarily because of its economic power. Germans are the leading foreign investors in several Eastern European countries. However, it seems that the physical presence of large German communities in the region is a thing of the past.

Gligorov, Kiro (1917–)

President of Macedonia, 1991–1999. Gligorov loyally served the Yugoslav Communist regime of Josip Broz Tito from the 1940s through the 1970s. Although a non-Communist nationalist coalition of political parties won a plurality in the parliamentary elections of late 1990, parliament nonetheless chose Gligorov to be the first president of Macedonia in January 1991. He quickly established himself as a moderate and sensible statesman, especially when it came to dealing with Macedonia's large Albanian minority. Gligorov was reelected to a new five-year term by popular vote in 1994, but was nearly killed in an assassination attempt in 1995. He heads a new political party formed in 1992, the Union of Macedonia, which is largely made up of reformed Communists like himself. Gligorov was a vital steadying force for his country during the 1990s.

Goncz, Arpad (1922–)

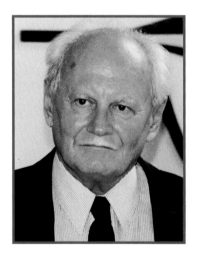

President of Hungary, 1990– . Goncz was trained as a lawyer. Before the Communist takeover of Hungary he was a leader of the conservative Independent Smallholders' Party. After the Communist takeover he was unable to practice his profession and worked as a welder and metalworker. Goncz was sentenced to life imprisonment for political activity in 1957, but was released under a general amnesty in 1963. He then earned a living as a freelance writer and translator. His publications include a novel, several plays, and a collection of short stories. In 1989, as the Communist regime disintegrated, Goncz was elected president of the Hungarian Writers' Union. He also was one of the founders of the Alliance of Free Democrats. He was elected president of Hungary in August 1990 and since then has established a reputation in political circles as a moderate.

Grigorievski, Ljubco (1966–)

Prime Minister of Macedonia, 1998– . Grigorievski received his university degree in comparative literature and is the author of two volumes of poetry and one short-story collection entitled *Direct Investments and Short Stories in the Anatomic Structure of History*. He played an active role in ending Communism in Macedonia and, at the age of twenty-five, served for eight months as his country's vice president. He resigned because he was dissatisfied with the slowness of the pace of reform toward democracy and a market economy. He led the Internal Macedonian Revolutionary Organization, a nationalist ethnic Macedonian group, to victory in the 1998 parliamentary elections. However, immediately after that triumph, Grigorievski took a major step toward closing the gap between his country's ethnic Macedonians and Albanians by inviting the leading Albanian political party to join his government, an offer that was accepted.

Gypsies

The Gypsies—or Romany as they prefer to be called—are a nomadic people who probably originated in northwest India. They seem to have begun their wanderings in the first century A.D. and since then have reached every continent. They probably arrived in Eastern Europe between the thirteenth and fifteenth centuries. They continued to stick together and speak

These Gypsies were part of the exodus from Kosovo during the 1999 war.

their own language, traveling in small caravans, although they usually adopted the religion of the majority people around them. Short, dark-skinned, and slightly built, they generally were physically distinct from the native populations of Eastern Europe. Gypsies earned their living in various ways. They were metalworkers and horse dealers, and also musicians, singers, dancers, and magicians. Gypsy women often were fortunetellers, some claiming they could communicate with the dead.

Gypsies were sometimes welcomed because of their skills and at times influenced the people around them. Franz Liszt (1811–1886), the great Hungarian composer, was strongly influenced by Gypsy music and culture and saw them as the creators of Hungarian national music. More often, however, Gypsies experienced bigotry and persecution, accused of everything from practicing sorcery and committing crimes to being unsanitary. That bigotry culminated in World War II when the Nazis murdered 500,000 Gypsies, mostly from Eastern Europe and Russia, in death camps. After the war, the Communist regimes, as part of their attempt to control all of society, at least provided some physical security for Eastern Europe's Gypsies. They also dramatically raised their low educational and literacy rates. For the first time, a Gypsy intelligentsia began to appear. At the same time, Communism was a confining straitjacket that ran counter to the Gypsies nomadic and spontaneous lifestyle.

The best guess is that there are at least 5 million Gypsies in Eastern Europe. Most Gypsies are extremely poor and still lack sufficient education. Although free from the restrictions imposed under Communism, Gypsies once again are victims of popular bigotry. They are especially vulnerable in economic hard times, when popular discontent leads to the search for easily identifiable scapegoats. One person who has risen to their defense is Czech President Vaclav Havel. Troubled by anti-Gypsy sentiments and acts in his country, he told the Czech people that a country is measured by what is "chanted by skinheads in a pub, by the number of lynched or murdered Romany people, by the dreadful behavior of some of our people toward their fellow humans simply because of the different color of their skin."[3] It is a message that most of its intended audience still has not heard.

Havel, Vaclav (1936–)

President of Czechoslovakia, 1989–1992; President of the Czech Republic, 1993– . Vaclav Havel was born in Prague into a prosperous family: His father was an architect, his mother the daughter of an established publisher, and his uncle the owner of a film studio. His family lost everything after the Communist takeover in 1948 and Havel, because of his "bourgeois" background, was denied a university education. After several years as a chemical laboratory technician and service in the military, he began work in the theater as a stagehand. It was not long before he established a reputation as a talented playwright and essayist. In the 1960s two of his plays, *The Garden Party* (1963) and *The Memorandum* (1965), both of which satirized Communism, received international recognition. Havel partici-

pated in the 1968 Prague Spring as president of the Club of Independent Writers and was banned from theater work in the reaction that followed. In 1977 he emerged as one of the leaders of the Charter 77 group formed to monitor Czechoslovakia's observance of the Helsinki human-rights agreements. Havel was arrested the next year, briefly released, and then arrested and imprisoned for more than four years, during which time he nearly died of pneumonia. By then he had a well-deserved reputation as a beacon of morality and courage that reached well beyond Czechoslovakia. He published one of his best-known essays, "The Power of the Powerless," in 1978. In it, he made the point that even in a totalitarian society individuals can resist and ultimately undermine tyranny by having the courage to be honest about their beliefs, or, as he called it, living "within the truth."[4] Havel's remarkable letters to his wife, Olga, while in prison were published as a book in 1988 (*Letters to Olga*).

Havel was not uncritical of the West, especially of its materialism. At the same time, he saw a fundamental moral difference between the democratic West and the totalitarian Soviet bloc and strongly criticized Western peace movements that ignored that difference. Along with other Eastern European dissidents such as Poland's Adam Michnik, Havel rejected the idea popular among intellectuals in the West in the 1970s and 1980s that the main threat to world peace was weapons, whether Western or Soviet. "What threatens peace in Europe," Havel wrote, "is not the prospect of change but the existing situation," that is, the existence of totalitarian regimes in Eastern Europe and the Soviet Union. Adam Michnik agreed, writing from his prison cell that Western peace advocates were wrong to think that "arms are more important than people. No weapon kills by itself."[5]

In 1989 Havel was one of the cofounders of Civic Forum, which led the nonviolent struggle that brought down the Communist regime. In December of that year he became Czechoslovakia's president, delivering a remarkable "New Year's Address" to his people in 1990. Havel frankly told his people: "We live in a contaminated moral environment" because under Communism "we became used to saying something different from what we thought. We learned not to believe in anything, to ignore each other, to care only about ourselves." The time had come, he added, to "teach ourselves and others that politics should be the expression of a desire to contribute to the happiness of the community rather than a need to cheat or rape the community."[6]

However, not even Havel's enormous moral authority could prevent narrow-minded ethnic politics from breaking up Czechoslovakia in 1993. He was in many ways out of his element when it came to the everyday rough-and-tumble politics of the post-Communist era. Still, Havel became the first president of the newly born Czech Republic, and was elected to a second five-year term in 1998. A heavy smoker, he survived surgery for lung cancer in 1996 and major intestinal surgery in 1998. After more than two decades in the public spotlight he never sought, this truly remarkable man remains the conscience of his country and an example of moral leadership on the international stage, providing a welcome contrast not only with Eastern Europe's fallen Communist leaders, but also with many politicians and national leaders in the democratic countries of the West.

Herbert, Zbigniew (1924–)

Polish essayist. Herbert was involved in the resistance to German occupation during World War II. He won international recognition for essays he wrote in the 1950s while on the staff of a literary journal in Warsaw. In 1974 he introduced a character in his writings named "Mr. Cogito," a man divided by conflicting values. Herbert sees human values as a "besieged city" in the modern world.

Holub, Miroslav (1923–)

Czech poet and essayist. Holub trained and worked as a physician before publishing his first collection of poems in 1958. After 1971 he was unable to publish his work in Czechoslovakia for more than a decade. His poetry and essays on science explore similar moral themes.

Horn, Gyula (1932–)

Prime Minister of Hungary, 1994–1998. Horn loyally served the Hungarian Communist Party from 1953 until the party renounced Communism and changed its name in 1989. He was, however, an advocate of reform, and as foreign minister in 1989 he made the public announcement that Hungary was opening its border with Austria to permit thousands of refugees from East Germany to go to the West. He played a major role in the Communist Party's effort to transform itself into a non-Communist socialist party and became the leader of the renamed Hungarian Socialist Party in 1990. As Hungary's prime minister from 1994 to 1998 he continued the policy of economic reform begun by the previous non-Communist government.

Hrabal, Bohumil (1914–)

Czech poet, novelist, and short-story writer. Despite his age, Hrabal in the 1990s has been one of Prague's literary stars. He lived a hard life under the Communist regime, earning his living as a steelworker until he was seriously injured in an accident. He later worked as a manual laborer and backstage in a theater. He probably is best known for his novella *Closely Watched Trains*, which in the 1960s was made into a highly successful film.

Iliescu, Ion (1930–)

President of Romania, 1990–1996. Iliescu began his association with Romania's Communist Party in 1944 as a member of its youth organization. He joined the party itself in 1953 and rose through the ranks until his split with Ceauşescu in 1971. However, he continued to serve in a number of official posts, including that of president of Romania's national council of water

resources. He also published several works on water resources and environmental protection. His election as Romania's president in 1990, and especially his reelection in 1992, disappointed many Western observers and Romanians committed to reform. Certainly, as president he permitted only limited reforms and behaved in an authoritarian manner. At the same time, Romania after Ceauşescu's fall was a very unstable country and, whatever Iliescu's many faults, his political skills may have kept the country from sliding into civil war. He thus probably should be viewed as a necessary transitional figure who did some good as well as harm.

Izetbegovic, Alija (1925–)

President of Bosnia 1990– . Izetbegovic has been accused by Bosnian Serbs and Croats of being an Islamic fundamentalist, a charge his supporters heatedly dispute. In the late 1960s Izetbegovic wrote the *Islamic Declaration*, a tract about the proper nature of an Islamic political system. Although this work did not specifically mention Bosnia (a wise tactic since Yugoslavia at the time was a Communist dictatorship), it

echoed many Islamic fundamentalist ideas and stamped Izetbegovic
as belonging to the religious rather
than secular wing of Bosnia's Muslim nationalist movement. Izetbegovic was imprisoned by
Yugoslavia's Communist dictatorship from 1983 to 1988 for what it
called Muslim nationalism and
"counter-revolution." In 1990, as
Yugoslavia was disintegrating, he
founded the Muslim Party for

Democratic Action under whose banner he became Bosnia's
president in 1990. Izetbegovic meanwhile worked to preserve
Yugoslavia by transforming it into a loose confederation, an
effort that ended in failure. By the mid-1990s, as Bosnia's Muslims reeled under attacks from both Serbs and Croats, Izetbegovic's views, along with those of other Bosnian Muslims,
appeared to harden. This reduced whatever chances he may
have had to genuinely serve as the president of all three Bosnian communities. In the 1996 presidential elections, won by
Izetbegovic, there were reports of harassment and violence
against Muslim opposition groups. One thing Izetbegovic
shares with most Serb and Croat leaders in Bosnia is coolness
toward the Dayton Accords.

Jews

The Jews have a long history in Eastern Europe. They came to
the Balkans in Greek and Roman times and arrived in parts of
Central Europe by A.D. 1000. Jews first settled in large numbers in Poland, where Europe's largest Jewish community
eventually developed, in the thirteenth century. They came as
refugees from persecution and expulsion in Western Europe

and because the Polish rulers welcomed them for their commercial and technical skills.

Since the Middle Ages European Jews never lived free of anti-Semitism and persecution. However, there were periods in various countries when anti-Semitism was at a low ebb and Jews were able to live in relative peace and prosperity. For several centuries Poland was the safest place in Europe for Jews, and Poland's Jewish community grew and developed until it was the demographic and cultural center of the Jewish world. During the late Middle Ages 80 percent of the world's Jews lived in Poland. In 1897, about 14 percent of Poland's population was Jewish. Because Jews concentrated in the towns, they made up an even larger percentage of Poland's urban population. In no other country outside their original homeland in what today is Israel did Jews ever amount to such a large percentage of the population.

During the Middle Ages the Jews in most of Eastern Europe lived in their own communities. They spoke their own language, Yiddish, which was based on medieval German but written with Hebrew letters. Education and the study of the Bible and the Talmud (a detailed commentary on the Bible) was the central focus of their lives and they produced thousands of outstanding scholars. They also played an important role in the economic life and development of the countries in which they lived. Beginning with the Enlightenment in the eighteenth century, when they were given the opportunity, Jews began to play a larger role in the secular life and culture of Eastern Europe. The list of Eastern European Jewish scientists, writers, musicians, artists, philosophers, doctors, lawyers, and businessmen who made significant contributions to European life is enormous.

About 6 million Jews lived in Eastern Europe before World War II. Almost all of them were murdered by the Nazis in the Holocaust. Most of the survivors emigrated, overwhelmed by the horrors that had befallen them and facing continued anti-Semitism from the local populations. The majority went to Israel. Today Eastern Europe's largest Jewish community, an estimated 80,000 people, lives in Hungary. Romania has about 14,500 Jews; perhaps 6,000 live in the Czech and Slovak Republics. About 3.3 million Jews lived in Poland in 1939. Ninety percent of them died in the Holocaust. Today only 5,000–6,000 declared Jews remain. There are thousands of additional Poles with Jewish ancestry—a reasonable guess is 30,000—who do not openly identify as Jews. Growing numbers of them—for a variety of reasons ranging from finally being told the truth of their ancestry to a desire to reclaim their heritage—are beginning to do so. They are doing so despite anti-Semitism that has resurfaced not only in Poland but also in other Eastern European countries since 1989. Among the causes of this revived anti-Semitism are extreme nationalist beliefs that are hostile to any "outsiders" and economic hardship that makes people look for simple answers and vulnerable scapegoats. A grim irony in all of this is that today's Eastern European anti-Semites have so few people to hate. Nothing can change the tragic reality that what is left after the Holocaust is a tiny remnant of the Jewish community that for more than a thousand years contributed so much to the life of Eastern Europe.

Johanides, Jan (1934–)

Slovakian novelist. During the 1970s the Czechoslovak Communist regime did not permit Johanides to publish his writing. Several of his books have been translated into Hungarian and German.

Kadare, Ismail (1936–)

Albanian novelist and poet. Under the Communist regime Kadare managed to get away with writing works that attacked Communist literary standards without being denied the right to publish. He is the only Albanian writer to win international recognition. His book *The General of the Dead Army*, published in the 1960s, is considered the first outstanding novel in the Albanian language. Since then he has produced several well-received novels. His works have been translated into many languages, including English.

Karadzic, Radovan (1945–)

Bosnian Serb leader. President of the internationally unrecognized Serb "republic" in Bosnia, 1992–1996, and president of the Serb Republic created by the Dayton Accords, 1996–1997. Karadzic was born and raised in Montenegro before moving to the Bosnian capital of Sarajevo as a teenager. He became a psychiatrist (he was the resident psychiatrist of the Sarajevo soccer team) and also was something of a poet. When Karadzic entered politics it was as an extreme Serb nationalist with a bitter hatred for Bosnia's Muslims. As the leader of the Bosnian Serbs he was responsible for their brutal policy of ethnic cleansing, for which the United Nations indicted him for war crimes in 1995. Attempts to capture Karadzic and bring him to trial were abandoned in July 1998, after two years of planning that cost $100 million, because of Western fears that such an attempt would lead to extensive violence and bloodshed. Karadzic still lives in Pale, a suburb of Sarajevo that was his headquarters during the Bosnian war.

Klaus, Vaclav (1941–)

Prime Minister of the Czech Republic (still part of Czechoslovakia), July-December 1992; Prime Minister of the independent Czech Republic, 1993–1997. An economist by training, Klaus worked with Vaclav Havel as chairman of the Civic Forum movement during 1990–1991. He then became the leader of the Civic Democratic Party, which advocated rapid

free-market reforms. Klaus disagreed with Vaclav Havel on several
issues, including the breakup of
Czechoslovakia, which Havel
strongly opposed, and Klaus, given
the Slovak opposition to a strong
central government, accepted as
the best of the available options. As
prime minister of the Czech
Republic, Klaus pushed for free-
market reforms. The Czech econ-

omy grew impressively in 1994 and 1995, and the country
attracted large amounts of foreign investment. However, economic growth slowed in 1996 and 1997, and Klaus had to take
the blame. He was criticized because many newly privatized
companies did not reorganize themselves, in part because they
were controlled by shady investment funds. In addition, Klaus
and his party were tainted by a scandal involving a secret Swiss
bank account. Although forced to resign as prime minister in
December 1997, Klaus remains a major figure in Czech politics.

Klima, Ivan (1931–)

Czech novelist, playwright, and short-story writer. Klima spent
three years in the Theresienstadt concentration camp during
World War II. He was part of a literary revival in Czechoslovakia when government controls were relaxed slightly in the early
1960s. Some of his work is strongly influenced by the great
Jewish-Czech writer Franz Kafka (1883–1924). Aside from
addressing themes such as people being repressed by the state
and their own lack of values, Klima in his recent work discussed
the problem of environmental destruction.

Konrad, Gyorgy (1933–)

Hungarian novelist and essayist. Konrad's themes include how
life in a totalitarian state destroys even those who are supposed
to benefit. He was for many years unable to get his work

legally published in Hungary and had to have it printed by underground presses or published abroad. His novel *The Loser* was published in English in 1982, a year before it appeared in Hungarian.

Koлovo

Province of Serbia with a predominantly Albanian population. Kosovo has an area of slightly more than 4,000 square miles (10,360 square kilometers). Prior to 1999 about 90 percent of its current population of 2 million were ethnic Albanians and 10 percent were Serbs. However, the province has deep historical importance for the Serbs. Many of the oldest Serbian Orthodox churches are in Kosovo, and it was the scene of the decisive Serbian defeat at the hands of the Ottoman Turks in 1389. In 1974, Yugoslav dictator Josip Broz Tito made Kosovo an autonomous province within Serbia. That status was revoked in 1989 by Slobodan Milosevic when Albanians openly began talking about independence. For the next several years Ibrahim Rugova and the Albanian Democratic League waged a nonviolent but persistent struggle for independence. They set up an underground government in 1992 that collected, by force when necessary, its own taxes. However, in 1993 more radical Albanians organized the Kosovo Liberation Army, which was committed to armed struggle, including acts of terror against Serb civilians. It launched a rebellion in 1998 that the Serbs met with massive military force. Tens of thousands of Albanians became homeless refugees as a result of the fighting.

In 1999 NATO intervened to stop brutal Serbian reprisals against Albanian civilians by bombing Serbia. The Serbs responded with a campaign of murder and mass expulsion that forced about 800,000 Albanians out of Kosovo. Most of the refugees returned after the Milosevic regime was forced to accept the occupation of Kosovo by 50,000 NATO troops. But two thirds of Kosovo's Serbian minority community of 200,000 fled the province. One of their fears, which turned out to be justified, was that NATO occupation forces would be unable to protect them from Albanian reprisals. These events left Kosovo mired in misery and NATO stuck with a expensive occupation with no end in sight.

Kostunica, Vojislav (1944–)

President of the Federal Republic of Yugoslavia, 2000– . Born in Belgrade in 1944, Kostunica graduated from Belgrade University Law School and later earned masters and doctorate degrees. His reputation for honesty and courage and his unquestioned credentials as a Serb nationalist enabled him to challenge and defeat Sloboday Milosevic in Yugoslavia's 2000 presidential elections.

Kovac, Michal (1930–)

President of the Slovak Republic, 1993–1998. Trained as an economist. Kovac was a member of the Communist Party of Czechoslovakia until being expelled after the Prague Spring. After parliament elected him president of the Slovak Republic in 1993, he opposed the dictatorial actions of Prime Minister Vladimir Meciar and became one of his country's voices of tolerance and moderation. During the 1994 parliamentary elections, he warned Slovak voters that elections:

> . . . should not turn into a life-or-death struggle, where the sole aim is the moral and political destruction of opponents. Let us remember that even after the election we will meet and cooperate with those whom we might have unnecessarily insulted . . . . Esteemed citizens! I would like to appeal to you to respect the results of the election even if your party or movement does not win or

achieve the results you hoped for. In a democratic system, the minority must accept the majority view and respect it. In some future election, the losers now may be winners, and it is therefore correct and proper that they respect each other.[7]

Kovac's plea went largely unheeded as Slovak politics grew increasingly nasty under Prime Minister Meciar. In 1998, when Kovac's term as president expired, the Slovak parliament was so divided that it was unable to elect a successor.

Krzaklewski, Marian (1950–)

Leader of Poland's Solidarity Union, 1990– . Krzaklewski, the son of a doctor, is a computer scientist by profession. When Lech Walesa left Solidarity in 1990 to run for president of Poland, Krzaklewski was elected to replace him as Solidarity's leader. Seven years later he was the main organizer of the Solidarity Action Alliance, a coalition of more than thirty groups that unexpectedly routed Poland's former Communists (the Democratic Left Alliance) in the parliamentary elections. Charismatic, strong-willed, and opinionated, Krzaklewski, like Walesa, believes the Roman Catholic Church should play a prominent role in Polish society.

Kucan, Milan (1941–)

President of Slovenia, 1990– . Kucan was trained as a lawyer and served the Yugoslav Communist regime for more than twenty years. However, he was an outspoken opponent of Slobodan Milosevic, the hard-line Serb leader whose policies contributed to the breakup of Yugoslavia. Kucan was elected Slovenia's president by parliament

in 1990, and then elected directly by the country's voters twice, in 1992 and again in 1997, to five-year presidential terms. His common-sense approach to politics helped keep his country on an even keel and made him the most successful national leader in any of the newly independent countries of the former Yugoslavia.

Kundera, Milan (1929–)

Czech novelist and essayist. Kundera established his reputation with his first novel, *The Joke*, a brilliant satirical attack on the dictatorial Communist system. He left Czechoslovakia after the 1968 Soviet invasion and settled in France. A writer of international renown, he explores the difficulties of finding fulfillment in the modern world. Kundera probably is best known for his novel *The Unbearable Lightness of Being*, which was made into a highly successful film.

Kwasniewski, Aleksander (1954–)

President of Poland, 1995– . Like Lech Walesa, the man he defeated in the bruising 1995 election, Kwasniewski has roots in the city of Gdansk, where he was a university student. He then worked as a journalist and later was a minister in Poland's Communist Regime. Unlike Walesa, Kwasniewski has a sophisticated image and is very articulate and restrained in his political behavior. He used that style to help reorganize Poland's former Communists into the Social Democratic Party of Poland, and then in 1991 organized a coalition of leftist parties called the Democratic Left Alliance, which won the 1993 parliamentary elections. As president, Kwasniewski continued to orient Poland's foreign policy toward the West and push for free-market reforms. He won reelection in October 2000.

Leka I (1939–)

Albanian monarchist. "King" Leka I was two days old in 1939 when his father, King Zog, fled the country after Italian fascist dictator Benito Mussolini invaded and occupied the country. In April 1997, fifty-eight years after his exile began, the would-be king visited his violence-stricken homeland, where more than five thousand people greeted him in his ancestral village 70 miles (113 kilometers) north of Tirana. Leka, who said he had come "to spread the message of peace and unity" called for a referendum on whether to restore the monarchy.[8]

Ljubljana

Capital and largest city (population 270,000) of Slovenia. Ljubljana traces its roots to Roman times, when it was called Emona. In 1277 it came under Hapsburg control (its German name is Laibach) and became a major provincial town. The Hapsburgs built many of the palaces, churches, and mansions that grace Ljubljana today. In the nineteenth century the city became a center of the Slovenian national movement. Today it is an industrial and transport center. More than 27,000 students attend Ljubljana University, giving the city something of the feel of a youthful college town.

Mejdani, Rexhep (1944–)

President of Albania 1997 – . A native of Tirana, Mejdani graduated first in his class with an honors degree in physics from

Tirana University and then went on to earn a doctorate. He had a distinguished academic career from the 1970s through the 1990s, serving as a visiting scientist, lecturer, and professor at several universities in Western Europe and the United States. In 1996 Mejdani joined the Socialist Party of Albania, the country's reorganized group of former Communists. He was chosen the party's general secretary that same year and elected to parliament in the June 1997 elections. Upon being elected president by parliament in July 1997, Mejdani resigned from parliament and the Socialist Party. His first priority as president clearly was to be conciliatory and bridge Albania's deep political divisions.

Meciar, Vladimir (1942–)

Prime Minister of Slovakia, 1990–1991, 1992; Prime Minister of Slovak Republic, 1993–March 1994, December 1994–1998. Meciar was educated as a lawyer and worked within Czechoslovakia's Communist establishment until he was expelled in 1970 as punishment for participating in the Prague Spring. He reemerged as a political figure in 1990 as a member of the Slovak group Public Against Violence, which was allied with Vaclav Havel's Civic Forum. However, Meciar soon turned to ethnic politics and was instrumental in the breakup of Czechoslovakia. As his country's prime minister he continued to play the ethnic card, including making inflammatory remarks about the Slovak Republic's 600,000-strong Hungarian minority, and became increasingly authoritarian. His years in power ended with his party's defeat in the 1998 parliamentary elections.

Mesic, Stipe (1934–)

President of Croatia, 2000– . Mesic served as a city mayor and member of the Slovakian parliament under the Communist regime before being imprisoned for a year in 1975 for advocating reforms. He remained out of politics until 1990. He then became a close ally of Franjo Tudjman and in 1992 became president of the Slovak Republic's parliament. Mesic then broke with Tudjman and became one of his most vocal critics. As a leader of the Croatian People's Party (HNS), one of the parties in the coalition that won

Slovakia's January 2000 parliamentary elections, Mesic was elected his country's president in February 2000.

Miloᴧevic, Slobodan (1941–)

President of Serbia, 1987–1997; President of the Federal Republic of Yugoslavia, 1997–2000. Milosevic was born in a small town southeast of Belgrade to recent immigrants from Montenegro. His father, who had once trained for the Orthodox priesthood, returned to Montenegro when Slobodan was nineteen and later committed suicide. His mother, a straitlaced Communist activist and teacher, also committed suicide. A central figure in Milosevic's life, both personally and politically, has been his wife, Mirjana Markovic. Both her parents were leading Communist political figures whose activities dated from World War II. She has been an important political figure in Yugoslavia in her own right and one of her husband's most effective supporters. Markovic, a newspaper columnist, is the leader of the Yugoslav United Left, a small political party allied with Milosevic's Socialist Party.

Milosevic rose through the Yugoslav Communist ranks as the protégé of Ivan Stambolic, who in 1986 became president of Serbia. In 1987 he sent Milosevic to Kosovo province to meet local ethnic Serb leaders. The Kosovo Serb community, a minority in the region where 90 percent of the population was ethnic Albanian, were increasingly concerned about Albanian assertiveness and acts of anti-Serb violence. Milosevic chose to inflame rather than calm the region's ethnic tensions. A militant speech he gave before a large Serbian crowd propelled him onto the national stage. The speech included the short sentence, "No one should dare to beat you," that electrified the angry and frightened crowd. The sentence "enthroned him as a Tsar," another Serbian leader reported. Several months later Milosevic pushed Stambolic aside and became Serbian president.[9]

Milosevic's militant and ruthless ethnic politics helped provoke the breakup of Yugoslavia and involved its successor, the Federal Republic of Yugoslavia (really just Serbia and Montenegro) in fighting with Croatia and the wars in Bosnia and Kosovo. All of this took a terrible toll on Serbia. In 1997, when barred from succeeding himself as president of Serbia, Milosevic engineered his election as Yugoslav federal president. This was a figurehead position, but under Milosevic that quickly changed. He was defeated when he ran for reelection in 2000.

Milosz, Czeslaw (1911–)

Polish poet, essayist, translator, and literary historian. Milosz is considered the greatest living Polish poet. He was born in Lithuania to an ethnic Polish family, lived in Warsaw during World War II, and was active in the underground against the occupying Germans. Although he left Poland after World War II, Milosz had enormous influence in his country with *The Captive Mind*, a study of corruption and dishonesty in political and literary thought and one of the classic intellectual rejections of Communism. Winner of the 1980 Nobel Prize for Literature, Milosz is one of the outstanding literary figures of the twentieth century. He has lived in the United States since the 1960s.

Orban, Otto (1936–)

Hungarian poet and translator. Orban was deeply scarred by the death of his Jewish father during the Holocaust. He grew up in an orphanage. He translated and was heavily influenced by the work of American "beat generation" poet Allen Ginsberg, and therefore became known as Hungary's "beat" poet. However, Orban also explored other themes and forms. A volume of his poetry was translated into English in 1993.

Orban, Viktor (1963–)

Prime Minister of Hungary, 1998–. When he was approved as prime minister by Hungary's parliament in July 1998, barely a month after his thirty-fifth birthday, Viktor Orban became the youngest prime minister in Europe. It was a dramatic change for Hungary, as Orban not only was replacing sixty-five-year-old Gyula Horn, one of Europe's oldest prime ministers but also a retread from the old Communist era. Orban and his Hungarian Civic Party (Fidesz), by contrast, were brand new. Orban was educated at England's Oxford University. Fidesz presented itself as the party of young entrepreneurs and the new middle class. It appealed to the middle class, but also to families, the working class, and the elderly, by going out on a limb and promising to cut taxes and abolish university tuition. The Fidesz campaign ran ads showing an athletic-looking Orban playing soccer with his young children. The party had a Web site in five languages. One of his top advisors even wears an earring. As one Fidesz official put it, "The people voted for youth, energy, dynamism, instead of the old guys, the used guys, the known guys."[10] That was true enough, but delivering on his campaign promises while maintaining steady economic growth was not going to be easy.

Paral, Vladimir (1932–)

Czech novelist. Paral was a chemist before turning to writing. During the 1960s and 1970s his books satirized the pursuit of power and privilege in Communist Czechoslovakia. In recent years he has looked with a critical eye at the pursuit of wealth in the capitalist Czech Republic. While critics rate Paral's books as serious literature, they also have a wide popular appeal.

Paskov, Viktor (1949–)

Bulgarian musician, screenwriter, and novelist. Paskov worked for several years as an opera singer, composer, and music critic in Germany. *Ballad for George Henig*, one of his three novels, was a best-seller in Bulgaria and won the French Grand Prix for literature. That book has been translated into English.

Plavsic, Biljana (1931–)

Bosnian Serb politician. Born in northern Bosnia, Biljana Plavsic rose to become dean of the department of biology at the University of Sarajevo. She also played an active role in Bosnian politics. During the civil war of 1992–1995 her visit to a frontline village led some supporters to call her the "Iron Lady," a label that well described her hard-line Serb nationalist views. Despite those views, the Western powers considered her the best available alternative to Radovan Karadzic, mainly because she was not personally corrupt and because she reluctantly accepted the Dayton Accords. In July 1996, after Karadzic was forced from office, Dr. Plavsic succeeded him as president of the Bosnian Serb Republic. However, she continually opposed the return of Muslim refugees to their homes in Serb-controlled areas, a violation of the Dayton Accords. In November 1997 her newly formed party, the Serb People's Alliance, was decisively defeated by Karadzic's Serb Democratic Action in local parliamentary elections. As one European diplomat glumly commented, "Plavsic has much less support than even we imagined."[11] In 1998 she lost her campaign for reelection to an ultra hard-line Serb nationalist.

Prague

Capital and largest city (population 1.2 million) of the Czech Republic. Prague is one of the most beautiful and elegant cities in the world. It was winning praise from travelers as early as the tenth century. In the fourteenth century, under the Holy Roman emperor Charles IV, who made Prague his imperial capital and built Eastern Europe's first university there, it was called the "Mother of All Cities." Goethe, the greatest poet of the German language, called it the prettiest gem in the stone crown of the world. Prague's extraordinary beauty is largely derived from three great eras of building, the first under Charles IV, the second under the Hapsburgs in the eighteenth century, and the third in the nineteenth and early twentieth centuries. The city's character was preserved because Prague did not become a battlefield during World War II and because the Communist regime did not "modernize" the city with hideous boxlike structures after the war. It says a great deal about the history of the Czech people that the two outstanding architects of the Hapsburg era who did so much to shape Prague were Germans, not Czechs. At the same time, the endless list of artists whose names are associated with the city— from Czech composers Bedřich Smetana and Antonin Dvõrák

The city of Prague

to the Austrian Wolfgang Amadeus Mozart to the Jewish writer Franz Kafka to President Vaclav Havel—attest to its enormously rich cultural traditions and cosmopolitan nature.

One of the less physically beautiful landmarks in the city, but one of the most historically significant, is Wenceslas Square. It is really not a square at all, but a long boulevard originally built by Charles IV as a horse market. Since then it has been the place where the Czechs have begun their great movements against foreign oppression and domestic despotism, from with the Hussite uprising of the fifteenth century to the Velvet Revolution of 1989, when hundreds of thousands of people rallied to bring down the Communist regime. Prague's symbol is the Charles Bridge, decorated with its famous promenade of sculptured saints, which spans the Vltava River that cuts through the center of the city. The bridge is not just a thoroughfare but a meeting place for Prague's residents and visitors alike.

Racan, Ivica (1944–)

Prime Minister of Croatia, 2000– . A longtime official in Yugoslavia's Communist Party, Racan belonged to the party's reformist wing. In 1990 he took the lead in forming the Social Democratic Party (SDP) out of the remnants of the collapsed Communist Party in Croatia. After the SDP's poor showing in the 1992 parliamentary elections, Racan gradually built the party into the strongest opposition group to Tudjman's Croatian Democratic Union (CDU). Racan then put together the alliance of opposition parties that defeated the CDU after Tudjman's death in Croatia's January 2000 parliamentary elections.

Radichkov, Yordan (1929–)

Bulgarian novelist, playwright, and screenplay writer. Radichkov is considered one of Bulgaria's outstanding literary figures. His novels have been translated into many languages and his plays are performed in Western Europe and the United States. Many of his characters are village people who are both frank and naive.

Rugova, Ibrahim (1944–)

Albanian leader in the Serbian province of Kosovo. Rugova studied in Paris, has a doctorate in literature, and is likely to quote William Shakespeare's *Hamlet* to help describe the tragic situation in his native Kosovo. Both his father and grandfather were executed in a 1945 uprising against the Communist Yugoslav regime. Rugova heads the Democratic League of Kosovo (LDK), which is dedicated to winning independence from Serbia. In 1992, after it organized underground elections, the Democratic League set up a shadow government in Kosovo, complete with schools, health services, and taxes. It was extremely risky for any Albanian family or business not to pay those taxes. Rugova was not arrested by the Serbian government primarily because he tried to avoid violence. He argued that time was on his side in a province where 90 percent of the population is Albanian and that vio-

lence would bring terrible reprisals. The prediction about the futility of violence came true in 1998 when a more radical Albanian group, the Kosovo Liberation Army (KLA), began an armed rebellion against Serbian control. That sparked brutal Serb repression, which, in 1999, in turn led to the NATO bombing war against Serbia and the Serbian campaign of murder and mass expulsion against the Kosovo's Albanian population. Although the NATO occupation of Kosovo restored an uneasy order to the province, the events of 1998–1999 saw Rugova and his LDK supplanted as the leaders of Kosovo's Albanians by Hashim Thaci and the KLA.

S

Sarajevo

Largest city (population 415,000) and officially the capital of Bosnia-Herzegovena. Sarajevo—the name comes from the Turkish word *sara*, or "palace"—was the city from which Turkish governors ruled Bosnia for four centuries. Local mosques and markets gave it a strong Turkish atmosphere, even after the Turks were driven from the city and Bosnia in 1878. In 1914, Sarajevo achieved dubious fame when the assassination of the heir to the Austrian throne by a Serbian nationalist became the incident that sparked World War I. It acquired a far more positive image as the host of the 1984 Winter Olympic Games. Inside Yugoslavia, Sarajevo was known as a place where Muslims, Serbs, and Croats lived together in peace. In 1991 its population was about 50 percent Muslim, 30 percent Serb, and 6.5 percent Croat. Sarajevo's cosmopolitan and tolerant atmosphere made it seem different from the rest of Bosnia. There even was a popular saying, "Goodbye Bosnia, I'm going to Sarajevo." The Bosnian civil war changed all that. The three-year Serb siege of the city reduced many sections to rubble and left more than ten thousand people dead. When the city was turned over to Muslim control by the Dayton Accords, most remaining Serbs and Croats left. Life in Sarajevo has been relatively normal since 1995, but the atmosphere of tolerance that made it a special place is gone, one of the many victims of the Bosnian civil war.

Schuster, Rudolf (1934–)

President of the Slovak Republic, 1999– . Schuster was educated as a civil engineer. He served as the major of the city of Kosice for three years during the Communist era. After the breakup of Czechoslovakia, Schuster served as the Slovak Republic's foreign minister from 1993 to 1994 and then as the mayor of Kosice from 1994 to 1998. In 1998 he became the leader of the newly founded moderate Party of Civic Understanding. He was elected his country's president in May 1999 and inaugurated the next month.

Shkreli, Azem (1938–)

Albanian poet, dramatist, and short-story writer. Shkreli is from Kosovo and represents the literary tradition of that province. Some of his writings have been translated into English.

Downtown Skopje, in Macedonia

Skopje

Capital and largest city of Macedonia (population 440,000). Skopje dates from Roman times. It was conquered by Serbia in 1282, and in 1346 was the city where the great Serbian ruler Stepan Dusan had himself crowned "tsar and autocrat of the Serbs, Greeks, Bulgarians, and Albanians." The city fell to the Turks in 1392 and remained in their hands until the Serbs retook it in 1912. In 1963 a severe earthquake killed more than a thousand people and destroyed large parts of the city. Much of the rebuilding that has shaped today's city was done in a sterile, oversize style. Located at a strategic point along the Vandar River, Skopje remains an important trade and industrial center.

Sofia

Capital and largest city in Bulgaria (population 1.2 million). Under various names, a city has existed where Sofia stands for more than two thousand years. It is located on a plateau in the geographic center of the Balkan Peninsula, about midway between the Adriatic and Black seas. Sofia thrived as a trading center for centuries until the Turkish conquest in 1382. After

The Nevsky Cathedral

five hundred years of Turkish rule, Sofia in 1879 became the capital of a newly autonomous Bulgaria. Badly damaged during World War II, the city was tastefully rebuilt after the war, with many open areas in the city center. Unlike many Eastern Europeans, the Bulgarians have warm feelings for the Russians, who drove the Turks from the country in 1878. A vivid testament to those feelings is the Alexander Nevsky Church, Sofia's largest. Completed in 1912, it honors the 200,000 Russian soldiers who died in the Russo-Turkish war of 1877–1878.

Sorescu, Marin (1936–1996)

Romanian poet, playwright, and painter. Sorescu's poems won him a wide audience in Romania, especially among the younger generation of poets. His plays rarely could get past Ceauşescu's censors, including one, *Vlad Dracula the Impaler*, that dealt with a brutally cruel medieval Romanian ruler. That play and several others have been translated into English.

Stoyanov, Petar (1953–)

President of Bulgaria, 1997– . Like his predecessor, Zhelyu Zhelev, Stoyanov is a firm anti-Communist. Unlike Zhelev, Stoyanov is known for his tact and welcoming discussion and dialogue. He campaigned for the presidency stressing the need for "reasonable change." Stoyanov also focused on winning the support of younger voters, telling them he was a guitar-playing member of the generation that came of age with the Beatles. His victory in the 1996 presidential elections, followed by the victory of the Union of Democratic Forces in

the 1997 parliamentary elections, were important steps toward reform in Bulgaria. Stoyanov's triumph, with almost 60 percent of the vote, was significant because he made inroads in many smaller towns and villages, which traditionally have supported the Bulgarian Socialist (former Communist) Party. Along with domestic reform, Stoyanov's priorities include moving Bulgaria closer to both the European Union and NATO.

Szabo Family (1959–)

Although a great deal has changed in Hungary since 1989, much less since 1959, one thing has not: The Szabos are still the country's first family. The Szabos are a fictional family whose life has been chronicled by an immensely popular radio program, *The Szabo Family*, which went on the air in 1959. The Hungarian government, anxious to make some kind of appeal to a population alienated by suppression of the 1956 uprising, asked a writer named Denes Liska to create a family radio drama. (Hungary had no television in those days.) Liska knew he had to tread a careful line. He avoided politics but did everything he could to reflect real life, including the problems of living in a Communist society. He succeeded brilliantly, and *The Szabo*

Family survived not only the collapse of Communism but the arrival of a large flock of television soap operas. Today the Szabos—some of whom are the "grandchildren" of the originals—deal with the problems of capitalism rather than Communism. Once they worked in state factories; today they run businesses. The also get divorced, criticize the corruption that accompanied privatization, and complain about the justice system. Liska still usually avoids politics. After forty years and more than two thousand episodes, the Szabos and their real-life problems are as popular as ever. As one actress on the show observed, "*The Szabo Family* is very much like the nation itself."[12]

Thaci, Hashim (1969–)

Leader of the Kosovo Liberation Army. As a young man Thaci belonged to a group committed to overthrowing Yugoslavia's government that was financed and backed by Enver Hoxha, the

Hashin Thaci assures an elderly Albanian woman that she would soon be able to return to Kosovo.

dictator of Albania until his death in 1985. Members of that group make up the core of the current KLA leadership. Thaci, whose nickname was "the Snake," became the leader of the KLA by using ruthless tactics that are notorious in the region against those who opposed him. Those tactics included kidnapping, torture, and execution. Thaci's goal remains to have Kosovo independent of Serbia, with himself as its leader.

Tirana

Capital and largest city of Albania (population 244,000). Tirana was founded in 1614 by a Turkish military governor. It developed into a craft center and in 1920 became Albania's capital. The fall of Communism changed the city's face. Its population rose as Albanians exercised their new right to live where they chose. Cafés selling Western drinks and discos blaring Western music opened, as did private restaurants. Until 1992 Tirana was unique among European capitals in that its street traffic was dominated by ox-drawn carts and bicycles, as it was illegal to own a private car in Albania. That changed with a vengeance when owning private cars became legal. Private cars—there were in Albania 20,000 by the summer of 1992 and 185,000 by 1993—brought mayhem to Tirana's streets. Reckless drivers raced, often without lights or even windshields, through the city's narrow, potholed streets at breakneck speed. Missing from today's Tirana is the huge statue of Enver Hoxha that once stood in the center of town; it was toppled after the collapse of Albania's Communist regime. The statue of Skanderbeg, still Albania's national hero, remains.

Tisma, Aleksandar (1924–)

Serbian poet and novelist. Tisma was born in Vojvodina, a region that before World War I belonged to Hungary. Like many people from that part of Serbia, Tisma is of mixed ethnic background—his father was a Serb and his mother a Hungarian Jew. Deeply scarred by the Holocaust and by the recent events in the former Yugoslavia, Tisma writes pessimistic fiction that explores why human beings are capable of terrible deeds. He is one of Serbia's few intellectuals prepared to discuss the questions of guilt, redemption, courage, and responsibility. He blames his country's misfortune on both its current crop of nationalist politicians and the former Communist regime that produced them. Yet he also assigns blame to opposition politicians and the population as a whole. In 1997 he grimly told a journalist, "People will not be happy for the next fifty years. No one has the courage to say we want to belong to the new order in the new world."[13] One of Tisma's novels, *The Book of Blam*, is being translated into English.

Trajkovski, Boris (1956–)

President of Macedonia, 1999– . Trajkovski was educated as a lawyer. He worked for many years as head of the legal department of a construction company in Skopje, Macedonia's capital city. Trakjovski is a Methodist in a country where most of the people are either Orthodox Christian or Muslim. During the Communist era in Yugoslavia he served for twelve  years as a leading official in the country's branch of the United Methodist Church. In 1998 he became a city official in Skopje and in 1998 became Macedonia's minister of foreign affairs. He was elected president of Macedonia in 1999.

Tudjman, Franjo (1922–1999)

President of Croatia, 1990–1999. Born in a small village near the Slovenian border, Tudjman fought with Tito's Communist Partisans in World War II, rising to the rank of general. After the war he served in Yugoslavia's defense ministry and on the Yugoslav Army's general staff. However, in the 1960s Tudjman rejected both Communism and the idea of a Yugoslav state and

became a militant Croat nationalist, increasingly hostile to Serbs. He was imprisoned for his nationalist beliefs in the 1970s, although he always received better treatment than other political prisoners. Upon his release, Tudjman continued to be treated better than other dissidents and was allowed to have a passport and travel abroad.

Tudjman published several books, some of them very controversial. His estimate that the fascist Ustashe regime killed "only" 60,000 Serbs, Jews, and Gypsies during World War II enraged many people, and is in fact less than one third of the generally accepted minimum figure. His book *Wastelands of History* contained anti-Semitic remarks that became an embarrassment once he was president of Croatia. In 1990 Tudjman caused a storm with the remark, "Thank God my wife is not a Serb or a Jew."[14] As Croatia's president, Tudjman continued to vigorously defend the Ustashe regime as a patriotic organization that helped pave the way for an independent Croatia and to honor officials who served in it. By 1997 his ethnic cleansing campaigns drove most Serbs from the country.

In recent years Tudjman attempted to sanitize his image by issuing a revised English edition of *Wastelands of History* (under the new title *Horrors of War*) with the anti-Semitic remarks edited out and by having the Croatian government apologize for Ustashe crimes against the Jews. These acts probably are best measured against Tudjman's overall conduct and view of history. As for democracy, after 1990 Tudjman made use of elections only when they served his purposes and violated democratic practices when they threatened his power. He died of stomach cancer in 1999, honored by many Croatians as the founder of their country but widely viewed elsewhere, and even by some Croatians, as a fanatic nationalist, destructive bigot, and corrupt and authoritarian politician.

Ugresic, Dubrakva (1949–)

Croatian novelist and essayist. Ugresic has published material that focuses on topics ranging from the nature of writing to the recent war in Croatia. She is also a serious student of modern Russian literature.

Vaculik, Ludvik (1926–)

Czech novelist and essayist. Vaculik was part of the 1960s literary revival in Czechoslovakia that included Milan Kundera and Vaclav Havel. His themes included the negative effects of Communism on rural life and the ecological dangers posed by industrialization. His recent work has generally been autobiographical.

Vilikovsky, Pavel (1941–)

Slovak fiction writer and translator. Vilikovsky was the coeditor of the most independent Slovak literary magazine during the 1970s and 1980s. Communist censorship delayed the publication of much of his work. He has translated the work of many famous foreign authors, including Virginia Woolf, William Faulkner, and Kurt Vonnegut.

Walesa, Lech (1943–)

Leader of Solidarity, 1980–1990; President of Poland, 1990–1995. In 1980 Lech Walesa was an unlikely hero. He was an unemployed electrician in Gdansk—he had been fired from his job for antigovernment protests—when a strike broke out in the city's Lenin Shipyard where he had once worked. Walesa climbed over the wall surrounding the yard and soon emerged as the leader of the striking workers. He displayed extraordinary skill and courage in dealing with the Polish government, both before and after its 1981 crackdown and imposition of martial law. In 1989 he negotiated the agreement in which the government again legalized Solidarity, and then led it to an overwhelming victory in the elections that followed. In 1990 he was elected president of Poland. Walesa's tenure as president certainly had important successes. Poland made a solid start in its transition from a Communist dictatorship to a democratic, free-market society. At the same time, Walesa probably stayed a bit too long at the center of Poland's political stage. He fought with both former Communists and his old Solidarity allies. Critics accused Walesa, a devout Catholic, of being too close to the Church hierarchy on contentious issues such as abortion. He was defeated in his 1995 bid for reelection. Still, whatever his shortcomings as Poland's president, Walesa will always be remembered as the steel-nerved electrician and union man who led Solidarity so brilliantly in such difficult circumstances.

Warsaw

Capital and largest city of Poland (population 1.64 million). Warsaw, Poland's cultural, industrial, and political center, straddles the country's most important river, the Vistula. It was founded in the fourteenth century as a stronghold for local dukes and became Poland's capital in 1596 after a fire devastated much of Cracow. Warsaw has been occupied and pillaged by conquerors several times in its history, but suffered by far its worst destruction during World War II. There were two dramatic and tragic uprisings in Warsaw during the war. The first occurred during April and May of 1943 when the Jews remaining in the Warsaw Ghetto—where the Germans had crammed 500,000 people into 2.4 percent of Warsaw's area before deporting them to the Auschwitz death camp—rebelled in the first civilian uprising against the Nazis in all of occupied Europe. Only a few hundred Jews survived the uprising and the

Old Town Square in Warsaw

Nazi reprisals that followed. The second uprising occurred between August and October of 1944, when the Polish resistance forces tried to take the city from the Germans. The Soviet army, only about a few miles to the east, stayed put as the Germans crushed the revolt and wiped out the core of Poland's non-Communist resistance movement. By the end of the war, 700,000 of Warsaw's citizens, including virtually all of its Jews, were dead, and 85 percent of its buildings were destroyed. No city in Eastern Europe suffered such devastating losses of life or property.

After the war, the Communist regime rebuilt much of Warsaw's medieval center—the *Stare Miasto*, or Old Town—including its fourteenth-century cathedral and marketplace, in its original form. The rest of the city was rebuilt along more modern lines. Its architecture ranges from dreary Stalinist structures to ultramodern steel and glass towers. Today Warsaw remains the heart of Poland, home to its Academy of Sciences, its International Chopin Competition, monuments to Copernicus and Adam Mickiewicz, the University of Warsaw, and historic churches and palaces.

Zagreb

Capital and largest city of Croatia (population 706,000). Croatia's capital since the sixteenth century, Zagreb grew out of two medieval towns, each centered on a Roman Catholic church. One of them, St. Steven's Cathedral, was destroyed by an earthquake in 1880; it was rebuilt and renamed the Cathedral of the Assumption of the Blessed Virgin Mary. The other, St. Steven's Church, is one of many medieval structures that still grace Zagreb today. Zagreb is in the part of Croatia that was never under Turkish con-

St. Stephen's Church

trol. It was a center of Croat nationalist activity during the nineteenth century and Yugoslavia's main industrial center before 1992. It suffered only minor damage during the fighting of 1992–1995 and today is an elegant and bustling city.

Zeman, Miloš (1944–)

Prime Minister of Czech Republic, July 1998– . Zeman was appointed after his Social Democratic Party won a plurality in the parliamentary elections in June 1998. Zeman's party is a left-center group whose roots lie in Europe's non-Marxist democratic socialist tradition. It rejects the strict free-market approach of Vaclav Klaus in favor of a stronger social safety net. Zeman favors increased welfare payments and a higher minimum wage, a slower pace of privatization, and tariff protection for local industries.

Zhelev, Zhelyu (1935–)

President of Bulgaria, 1990–1997. Zhelev, born into a peasant family, was an early beneficiary of Communist social policies when he was given the opportunity to study philosophy at Sofia University. He joined the Communist Party, but was bitterly disappointed in the limited reforms after Stalin's death and turned against Communism. Before he could finish his doctorate—he stunned everyone by writing a thesis critical of Lenin—Zhelev was expelled from the party and the university and forced to leave Sofia. He endured many hardships before finally being allowed to earn his doctorate. In the early 1980s he completed *Fascism*, the book that made him famous. It drew clear parallels between fascism and Communism as totalitarian ideologies. In 1988, inspired by Mikhail Gorbachev, Zhelev founded the Club for Glasnost and Perestroika. The next year protesters waved and held aloft *Fascism* as they demonstrated during the last days of Communist rule. After Todor Zhivkov was removed from office by fellow Communists, Zhelev became the leader of the opposition coalition Union of Democratic Forces. He was elected Bulgaria's president by parliament in 1990. In 1992, he was elected directly by the people to a four-year term. However, Bulgaria's social, economic, and political problems undermined his popularity and he was not reelected. Zhelev remains, however, a highly respected figure in Bulgaria. His book *Fascism* continues to sell; an English edition was published in Sofia in 1997.

Notes

Chapter One

1. *Congressional Record*, 78th Congress, Second Session, 1946, pp. 1145-1147.
2. Quoted in Jaques Rupnic, "Central Europe or Mitteleuropa?," in Stephen R. Graubard, ed., *Eastern Europe . . . Central Europe . . . Europe* (Boulder, CO: Westview Press, 1991), p. 235.

Chapter Two

1. Dean S. Rugg, *Eastern Europe* (London and New York: Longman, 1985, p. 21.
2. *The New York Times*, December 22, 1989.
3. *The New York Times*, March 29, 1997.
4. *The New York Times*, September 21, 1997.
5. *Ibid*.
6. *The New York Times*, March 13, 1999.

Chapter Three

1. Eva Hoffman, *Exit Into History: A Journey Through the New Eastern Europe* (New York: Viking, 1993), p. 216.

2. Imre Nagy, Radio Announcement of November 4, 1956, in Robert V. Daniels, ed., *A Documentary History of Communism and the World: From Revolution to Collapse* (Hanover and London: University Press of New England, 1994), p.173.
3. *The New York Times*, November 17, 1997.
4. *The International Herald Tribune*, May 28, 1998.
5. *Ibid.*
6. *The New York Times*, September 6, 1997.
7. *The International Herald Tribune*, May 26, 1998.

Chapter Four

1. Ivan Klima, "The State of Europe," in Lyman H. Legters, ed., *Eastern Europe: Transformation and Revolution, 1945-1991. Documents and Analysis* (Lexington, MA: D.C. Heath, 1992), p. 362.
2. Vaclav Havel, "New Year's Address," in Vaclav Havel, *Open Letters: Selected Writings, 1965-1990*, selected and edited by Paul Wilson (New York: Knopf, 1991), p. 300,
3. *The New York Times*, December 12, 1997.
4. *Ibid.*
5. *The New York Times*, November 4, 1999.

Chapter Five

1. Quoted in Milton F. Goldman, *Revolution and Change in Central and Eastern Europe: Political, Economic, and Social Challenges* (Armonk, NY: M.E. Sharpe, 1997), p. 282.
2. *The New York Times*, November 18, 1996.
3. *The New York Times*, November 19, 1996.
4. *The New York Times*, January 15, 1997.
5. *The New York Times*, May 8, 1997,
6. *The New York Times*, May 22, 1998.
7. Quoted in Raymond Zickel and Walter R. Iwaskiw, eds., *Albania: A Country Study* (Washington, D.C.: Federal Research Division, Library of Congress, 1994), p, 12.
8. *The New York Times*, July 25, 1997.

Chapter Six

1. *The New York Times*, May 21, 1997.
2. The *New York Times*, December 20, 1997.

3. The *New York Times*, April 12, 1997.
4. *U.S. News & World Report*, July 21, 1997, p. 40.
5. *Ibid*.

Encyclopedia
1. *The New York Times*, December 10, 1997.
2. *The Economist*, May 3, 1997.
3. *The New York Times*, December 12, 1997.
4. Vaclav Havel, "The Power of the Powerless," *Open Letters: Selected Writings, 1965–1990*, selected and edited by Paul Wilson (New York: Knopf, 1991), p. 150.
5. Quoted in Timothy Garton Ash, *The Uses of Adversity: Essays on the Fate of Central Europe* (New York: Random House, 1989), p. 197.
6. Vaclav Havel, "New Year's Address," in *Open Letters*, pp. 391, 395.
7. Quoted in Carol Skalnik Leff, *The Czech and Slovak Republics: Nation Versus State* (Boulder, CO: Westview Press, 1997), pp. 105–106.
8. *The New York Times*, April 21, 1997.
9. Quoted in Tim Judah, *The Serbs: History, Myth, and the Destruction of Yugoslavia* (New Haven and London: Yale University Press, p. 162.
10. *The New York Times*, June 5, 1998.
11. *The New York Times*, December 8, 1997.
12. *The New York Times*, January 24, 1998.
13. *The New York Times*, August 8, 1997.
14. Quoted in Laura Silber and Allen Little, *Yugoslavia: Death of a Nation* (New York and London: Penguin, 1995), p. 86.

Index

Page numbers in *italics* refer to illustrations.

D

P